CONTENTS

How to use this book

The *Beginner's Guide* series aims to introduce readers to major writers of the past 500 years. It is assumed that readers will begin with little or no knowledge and will want to go on to explore the subject in other ways.

BEGIN READING THE AUTHOR

This book is a companion guide to Milton's major works. It is not a substitute for reading the texts themselves. It would be useful if you read some of the works in parallel, so that you can put theory into practice. This *Beginner's Guide* is divided into sections. After considering the relevance of Milton today and a brief biography, we go on to explore some of Milton's main writings and themes before examining some critical approaches to the author. The survey finishes with suggestions for further reading and possible areas of further study.

HOW TO APPROACH UNFAMILIAR OR DIFFICULT TEXTS

Coming across a new writer such as Milton may seem daunting, but do not be put off. The trick is to persevere. Much good writing is multi-layered and complex. It is precisely this diversity and complexity which makes literature rewarding and exhilarating.

Literary work often needs to be read more than once, and in different ways. These ways can include: a leisurely and superficial reading to get the main ideas and narrative; a slower, more detailed reading focusing on the nuances of the text, concentrating on what appear to be key passages; and reading in a random way, moving back and forth through the text to examine such things as themes, narrative or characterization.

VOCABULARY

You will see that key words and unfamiliar terms are set in **bold** text. These words are also defined and explained in the glossary to be found at the back of the book.

You can read this introductory guide in its entirety, or dip in wherever suits you. You can read it in any order. It is a tool to help you appreciate Milton. We hope you enjoy reading it and find it useful.

Rob Abbott and Charlie Bell
Series Editors

Why read Milton Today?

Approaching *Paradise Lost* for the first time can be daunting. Its sheer size can be off-putting, let alone its grand themes of God, freedom, evil and moral responsibility. You might be surprised to discover how endlessly fascinating the poem is, and how it can speak to us just as it has spoken to every generation since it was first published over 300 years ago.

HIS MASTERY OF THE ENGLISH LANGUAGE IS UNSURPASSED

In reading Milton today, we quickly become aware of that which has, for many, made him one of the most compelling writers in English: his sheer mastery of language. In Milton there is nothing merely ornamental; every word earns its keep. Among his triumphs of language is Milton's ability to employ unsophisticated words to convey a sense of incomprehensible mystery. Take, for example, his description of Death in the second book of *Paradise Lost*, in which chiefly simple, monosyllabic words are used, to powerful effect:

> The other shape,
> If shape it might be called that shape had none
> Distinguishable in member, joint, or limb,
> Or substance might be called that shadow seemed.
>
> (*Paradise Lost*, II, 666–9)

The illustration is sublime and riddling yet expressed in the simplest of terms. The poet and critic Matthew Arnold later called this form of expression Milton's 'grand style' (*Essays in Criticism*, London, 1908). Such a talent for making language sing in its simplicity and yet still contain the immensity of his thought is among Milton's greatest achievements.

EVERY IMPORTANT WRITER AFTER MILTON WAS INFLUENCED BY HIM

Just as Milton's work, especially his *Paradise Lost*, speaks to our situation, it has never failed to address other generations on their own terms. It is this durability that is the hallmark of Milton's greatness. While his decision to write *Paradise Lost* in unrhymed blank verse occasioned plenty of criticism at the time, writers as diverse as Andrew Marvell and Alexander Pope rallied to express their awe at Milton's devastating poetic power.

Yet Milton's grand style evoked as much anxiety as admiration from succeeding generations of writers. Many poets found themselves trying to imitate this style while others faulted themselves for failing to achieve such grandeur. Among the most influential aspects of his writing was the Miltonic inversion, or the reversal of normal word order (as with Milton's description of Death whose 'shape had none'). So strong was his unique voice in the ears of later writers, that even the Romantic poets felt stifled by his influence. Keats, for one, once abandoned several hundred lines he had begun of a poem entitled *Hyperion* because it sounded too much like Milton: '... there were too many Miltonic inversions in it' (Letter to John Hamilton Reynolds, September 21, 1819).

MILTON POIGNANTLY ADDRESSES THE PROBLEMS OF HUMAN SUFFERING AND PAIN

The questions that moved Milton's imagination can be stated very simply: how can it be that an omnipotent and wholly good God would allow human suffering to exist? If God is all-powerful and does not intervene in human affairs to stop pain or anguish, can he really be said to be good? If God is totally good and abhors watching his creation suffer, does it not follow that he is powerless to stop it? Milton's stated aim in writing *Paradise Lost* was to construct an answer to these questions. The poem was written, he said, to 'assert Eternal Providence/ And justify the ways of God to men' (*Paradise Lost*, I, 25–6). In a world where human pain and suffering continually baffle and beset us, Milton sought to offer his own understanding of God's role in the world.

To answer these questions, Milton looks to the Creation story encapsulated in the first few paragraphs of the Bible, in the book of Genesis: the story of God's creation of the world and of Adam and Eve; his commandment that they should not eat fruit from the Tree of Knowledge; and their disobedience and subsequent expulsion from the garden of Eden. Known generally as the Fall from Eden, this story acts as the basis of Milton's analysis of suffering in *Paradise Lost*. Just as Adam and Eve lose their paradise by disobeying God's command, so we, through our free acts, render the world a fallen, painful place to live. For Milton, it is we and not God who are responsible for suffering and pain; through our God-given free will we conspire to destroy our own happiness.

HIS IDEAS ABOUT HUMAN FREEDOM AND RESPONSIBILITY SPEAK TO OUR SOCIETY'S APATHY

In the cut and thrust of today's society individuals often find themselves reduced in some way. Our class, sex, race or financial situation can all be used as labels to determine where we should live, whom we should marry and how we should vote. Defeating these expectations has been the peculiar task of twentieth-century men and women; yet the poetry of Milton, a seventeenth-century radical, has much to offer to our continued struggle for racial, sexual and material freedoms. Milton strongly believed in the power of human free will to overcome the determining factors of life. This idea is often referred to as Milton's libertarianism and can still be seen as a challenge to the way we view ourselves in the twenty-first century.

Milton not only wrote poetry but also radical political and religious tracts, which proved to be enormously influential on his peers. In one of his earlier tracts, *The Reason of Church Government* (1642), Milton writes of his determination 'to lay up as the best treasure, and solace of a good old age ... the honest liberty of free speech'. Milton's insistence, both in *Paradise Lost* and in his other poems, is thus that we do not need to be passively determined by our situation; we are, for the most part, as free or constrained as we choose to be.

* * *SUMMARY* * *

We should explore Milton's work today because:

● his mastery of the English language enabled him to express sublime and mysterious intuitions in the in the simplest of terms;

● his poetry has had such a profound influence on successive generations of writers, particularly the Romantic poets;

● his attempt to address the problem of pain has much to say to a suffering world;

● his assertion of human free will speaks to our society's apathy.

Biography 2

In his book *Opium* (1933), Jean Cocteau writes: 'I wonder how people can write the lives of poets, since the poets themselves could not write their own lives. There are too many mysteries, too many true lies, too many entanglements'. In Milton's case, such mysteries and fictions have been plentiful; the poet himself often wove tantalizing autobiographical details into his works and very soon after he died competing accounts of his life began to appear in print. Although no one account can recapture the man as he really was, we are fortunate enough to have access to Milton's mind not only through his published works but also through his letters, his early academic exercises and the reminiscences of those who actually knew him. Having so much material at our disposal, it is possible to think of Milton in many different guises: not only as the sublime poet but also as the forceful statesman, the scholar, the advocate, the theologian and the political idealist.

John Milton was born in Bread Street, London, on Friday 9 December 1608. His father, also John, had been disinherited by Milton's Roman Catholic grandfather for becoming a Protestant. Making his way to London, John Milton senior made good by becoming a scrivener, an extremely lucrative profession that included the offices of scribe, accountant, private banker and investment broker. We know little else about the poet's mother Sara other than that she was the daughter of a merchant tailor and, by the poet's own account, much admired for her charitable works. John senior and Sara had four children, three of whom survived: John junior, Anne and Christopher.

EARLY YEARS AND EDUCATION
By all accounts the young John Milton was a precocious and studious little boy who had loving parents, and a somewhat over-pampered

childhood. In his own account of his boyhood years, Milton writes that his father intended great things for him from the beginning: 'My father destined me … for the study of humane letters, which I seized with such eagerness, that from the twelfth year of my age I scarcely ever went from my lessons to bed before midnight' (*Defensio Secunda*, 1654). Milton was later to attribute the early cause of his blindness to these midnight study sessions. As well as having private tutorials at home, the young Milton entered a famous Cathedral school where as one of the so-called 'pigeons' of St Paul's he was to learn Latin, Greek and Hebrew.

Aged only 16, Milton was admitted to Christ's College, Cambridge, as a student under tutor William Chappell. By all accounts, Milton's life at Cambridge was colourless in comparison to his time at St Paul's. Academically, John was way ahead of the other students and resented having to follow an old-fashioned curriculum which focused on logic, rhetoric and ethics. While his fellow students nicknamed him 'The Lady of Christ's' on account of his delicate features, clear skin and haughty behaviour, Milton also had some kind of disagreement with his tutor and, so the story goes, was temporarily suspended, having to undergo the indignity of returning briefly to his parents' house. Milton's brother Christopher started the rumour that John had suffered corporal punishment at Chappell's hand by relating to a contemporary biographer that Milton had undergone 'some unkindnesse' from Chappell. The biographer, John Aubrey, suggestively added in the margin two words: 'whip't him'. (John Aubrey, 'Minutes of the Life of Mr John Milton' in Darbishire, Helen, 1932 *Early Lives of Milton*). Whether the legend has any credibility or not, or whether Milton returned home simply to escape the threat of plague in Cambridge (it is impossible to know for sure), he returned to Cambridge under the supervision of a different tutor, Nathaniel Tovey, and was soon to earn the respect of the other students as well as graduating on time.

Following completion of his MA at Cambridge in 1632, Milton removed first to his father's property in Hammersmith, and then to the new family home in Horton near Windsor in order to devote himself to an intense period of private study and reflection. This extended interval of self-education in history, theology, literature and philosophy, over five years in all, was eventually to give Milton the preparation necessary to write *Paradise Lost*. In these years, the poet would decide against a church career, preferring instead to continue his programme of reading and writing. In 1634 Milton was to write *Comus*, a masque for public performance on the theme of chastity. In 1637, following the drowning of his contemporary at Cambridge, Edward King, the young Milton would compose one of his most beautiful and strange poems on the themes of love and loss, *Lycidas*. A pastoral elegy, *Lycidas* has all the hallmarks of Milton's later 'grand style': poise, complexity, range of reference, and psychological acuity.

PERSONAL AND POLITICAL UPHEAVAL

The year 1637 was to be one of tremendous change for the poet. As well as confronting the loss of Edward King, Milton also had to contend with the death of his mother and that of his **patroness** the Countess of Derby. His great sense of personal loss, as well as his unease

KEYWORD

Patroness: One who uses her money and influence to support worthy people.

with the rising political tension in England as the dictatorship of the monarchy came into open conflict with radical Protestantism (see Historical, political and religious contexts), led Milton to reassess what his future role in English society should be.

In order to think about his future place in such a divided society, Milton embarked upon a 15-month trip to France, Italy and Geneva. By all accounts, Milton enjoyed a level of popularity in Europe that he would not experience in England until he was an old man. Appearing as the guest of honour at the houses of the finest continental noblemen and scholars, Milton was able to find the intellectual companionship that he had craved and lacked at Cambridge. He wrote of that time: 'There I quickly contracted intimacy with many truly noble and learned men. I also assiduously attended their private academies, an institution which is most highly to be praised there, not only for preserving the arts but also for cementing friendships' (*The Life Records of John Milton*, J. Milton French, ed. 1949–58).

As well as indulging his tastes for fine art, music, theatre and architecture, Milton was able to meet some of the most eminent men of his age. Visiting the astronomer Galileo in Florence, 'grown old a prisoner to the Inquisition, for thinking in astronomy otherwise than the Franciscan and Dominican licensors thought' (*The Life Records of John Milton*), must have led Milton to reflect upon the tyrannies of Archbishop William Laud back in England. Laud regularly removed the ears of those who dared disagree with his vision of religious orthodoxy.

Having travelled through Catholic Italy to Protestant Geneva on his slow journey home, Milton met the great Calvinist theologian Giovanni Diodati, uncle of his best friend at Cambridge, Charles Diodati. It was probably here that Milton learned of Charles' death in the previous August and A. N. Wilson writes that 'Milton's life, from now on, has some of ... (the) quality of widowhood' (*The Life of John Milton*). Soon afterwards, when Milton realized that political events in England had now come to a head – King Charles was attempting to force the Scottish clergy to accept Episcopal liturgy – the poet returned home through France to take up his destiny as one of the most prominent spokesmen for what would soon become the English republic.

MILTON AND FREEDOM

In 1639 Milton returned from the Continent and settled into a house in London. He began to earn a living by teaching his nephews and embarked on the self-appointed task of political pamphleteering for the Republican cause, advocating both religious freedom and universal education. The fast-maturing poet characterized his entry into public life as 'embark[ing] in a troubled sea of noises and hoarse disputes'

(*The Reason of Church-Government*). Yet his allegiance to the Republican cause was by no means unqualified: Milton refused to compromise on his own ideals in the interest of politics. In 1644 the poet published a potentially explosive treatise, *Areopagitica*, following the Commons' decision to censor and control all publications. In it, Milton raises an impassioned argument for the importance of freedom of speech, famously proclaiming:

> As good kill a man as kill a good book; who kills a man kills a reasonable creature, God's image; but he who destroys a good book kills reason itself, kills the image of God, as it were, in the eye.

This must have been a difficult time for Milton, committed to the Cromwellian cause and yet unwilling to agree with all of their actions. Imprisonment, or worse, had become a real possibility.

MARY POWELL

Eyebrows were raised when in 1642, aged 33, Milton returned from a short business visit to Oxfordshire with a beautiful and delicate 17-year-old bride, Mary Powell. Mary, the eldest daughter of Royalist squire Richard Powell, who owed money to Milton's father, was quickly married to Milton and moved with him back to London. However, it was only one month later when the teenage bride returned to her parents' house in Oxfordshire, flatly refusing to come back even when her husband sent for her. Edward Phillips, Milton's nephew and former pupil, writes that he was himself turned away from the Powells' house 'with some sort of Contempt' (*The Early Lives of John Milton*).

No one knows exactly why Mary renounced married life with Milton so quickly, although the incident has provoked plenty of speculation from both critics and biographers of the poet. We do know that Mary came from a large and boisterous family; Phillips tells us that it was Milton's 'philosophical life' (*ibid*) to which his new wife could not adjust. We also know that Mary's character differed markedly from that of her husband; her lack of education and interest in literature or religion must have quickly bored the scholarly young Milton. Perhaps the deciding factor in the separation was political: Mary's family were staunch Royalists while Milton was an avowed Independent. As the political temperature was rising in England (see Historical, political and religious contexts), London was becoming more dangerous for Royalist supporters and it is possible that Mary's family had become afraid for her safety.

After his wife's withdrawal, Milton quickly began publishing on the subject of divorce. Between 1643 and 1645, Milton wrote four notorious tracts against then current divorce law, which allowed couples the right to divorce only in cases of adultery. In Milton's opinion, simple incompatibility was a more valid ground for divorce; he argued that God's harmony in creation was undermined by an unhappily married couple with 'incoherent and uncombining dispositions' (*Doctrine and Discipline of Divorce*, 1643). Whatever his personal reasons for writing in this way (and we cannot seriously doubt that he had them), it did take an extraordinary amount of courage to rethink such inherited moral laws. Milton would have been aware that, without the formal backing of any party at this stage, he was courting disapproval from the Puritans in Parliament, the Church and Royalist supporters alike.

Some time in 1645, Milton's friends engineered a reunion between the couple. The Miltons were reconciled and, within a year, their first child Anne was born, followed by Mary in 1648, John in 1651 (he died after only 15 months), and Deborah in 1652. Mary Milton would herself die only a few days after Deborah was born.

Milton married twice more before he died, once to Katherine Woodcock in 1656, who died of childbirth complications only 14 months after the wedding, and once to Elizabeth Minshull in 1663, who outlived the poet.

DEPRESSION AND BLINDNESS

In 1652 Milton – publicly maligned by political antagonists, grieving for his wife and son, and by now totally blind (his eyesight had been gradually fading for years) – became temporarily but severely depressed. In a letter to a friend, describing the symptoms of his failing sight, Milton wrote: '... as my sight became daily more impaired, the colours became more faint, and were emitted with a certain inward crackling sound; but at present ... there is diffused around me nothing but darkness, or darkness mingled and streaked with an ashy brown' (*The Life Records of John Milton*). While the cause of Milton's blindness is not known, possible reasons include a brain tumour, cataracts, glaucoma and even congenital syphilis.

MILTON AS A PUBLIC SERVANT (1649–60)

Soon after the execution of Charles I in 1649, Milton published an unsolicited political tract defending the regicide, *The Tenure of Kings and Magistrates* (see Historical, political and religious contexts). Following its publication, Oliver Cromwell swiftly approached Milton with the offer of a role in governing the new republic and Milton readily agreed, working first as the Secretary for Foreign Languages in Cromwell's Council of State (acting as an interpreter, translator and author of tracts defending acts of the republic) and then as Chief Censor. This last post represents an ironic turn of fortunes for the poet who had so eloquently defended the right to free speech in *Areopagitica*. Milton, to his credit, appears to have been extremely permissive in his interpretation of the texts that came before him.

Yet the practicalities of government proved more difficult for many in the Cromwellian republic. By the late 1650s, around the time when his work on *Paradise Lost* had begun in earnest, Milton's dream of a Protestant republic was turning into a nightmare. The regime was fatally flawed with factions and instability and by 1660, when Charles II returned to England, the country became a monarchy again. As feared, the new monarchy was just as restrictive as the old: Milton was forced into hiding with friends, his writings were publicly burned by the official hangman, and he was arrested, briefly imprisoned and fined. It is likely that it was only his friendship with prominent Royalists (including his brother Christopher, the playwright Sir William Davenant, and the poet Andrew Marvell) that saved him from execution.

RETIREMENT, ILL HEALTH AND DEATH

After the Restoration, Milton found himself financially and physically crippled. Although he had difficulty paying for books or for people to take dictation from him, he managed to complete his three major poetic masterpieces, *Paradise Lost*, *Paradise Regained* and *Samson Agonistes* in the few years before he died. Apparently the ageing poet would compose verse in his head at night, waiting, as he called it, 'to be milked' in the morning by his nephews, daughters, friends and assistants.

When *Paradise Lost* was published in 1667 it quickly became one of the best sellers of the century. Recognized by critics as one of the most important poems ever to be written in English, Milton became a much celebrated figure. When, aged 65, the poet finally died of gout, it happened so peacefully that nobody in the room was aware that he had passed away.

Historical, political and religious contexts

3

It would be difficult to name another writer whose biography, social history, political temperament and religious convictions were more interlaced into the fabric of his writings than those of John Milton. In order to understand more fully the complexity of Milton's poetry, we shall explore in this chapter some of the momentous social, political and religious upheavals that occurred in England both before and during his lifetime. Central to this period, and to Milton's life and writing, was the English Civil War – arguably the most profound event in English political history.

ENGLAND IN THE SIXTEENTH CENTURY

After 1534, during the European **Reformation**, Henry VIII destroyed the Catholic monasteries in England and created a national **Protestant** church, the Church of England. By doing so, the King effectively severed England from the rule of Roman Catholicism under the Pope. In the years following this change and leading up to the birth of Milton in 1608, England saw as many fundamental religious changes as she saw monarchs to institute them. Edward VI, Henry's son, continued the reform of religion in England, deterring the use of iconography in the churches and sanctioning the dissemination of Protestant doctrine from the pulpits. After Edward's death in 1553, he was succeeded by his half-sister Mary Tudor, a Catholic who would not only overturn much of his reform, but would even go so far as to burn professing Protestants at the stake.

KEYWORDS

Reformation: a complex of events and movements in the sixteenth century instigated by a German priest, Martin Luther, and aimed at reforming the Roman Catholic Church.

Protestant: an umbrella term referring to the Christian denominations emerging in opposition to Roman Catholicism during the Reformation. Included within it in Milton's time were the Puritan, Presbyterian and Independent sects.

In a turn of events that alleviated many of these religious and political tensions, Elizabeth I, known as the Virgin Queen, succeeded her sister Mary. Elizabeth promoted what she called a 'middle way' between Catholic and Protestant doctrine and practice in the churches, asking only for superficial religious conformity. Following Elizabeth's death in 1603, the Scottish king James VI ascended the throne. Although both countries were Protestant nations, religious tensions remained high as divisions *within* Protestantism began to open up. The Scottish opposed the rule of Bishops within the Church, known as the Episcopacy, while the more moderate English Anglicans favoured this structure. These theological differences contributed significantly to the events that would end in civil war.

By the time that Charles I succeeded to the throne in 1625, when Milton was 17 years old, religious dissension and political dissatisfaction had reached fever pitch within Britain. Like James before him, Charles would prove unable to manage either the delicate balance of supremacy between Crown and Parliament or the plethora of conflicts between his Catholic and Protestant subjects regarding their religious freedom. Unlike James, though, Charles I was destined to see these conflicts through to the bitter end in his own lifetime.

THE ORIGINS OF CIVIL WAR

Charles I's attempt to impose the Anglican prayer book on the Scottish Church in 1637 aggravated Parliament. His refusal to come to the aid of other Protestants in Europe during the Thirty Years War embittered the Church. But it was Charles's unpopular decision to allow the Archbishop of Canterbury, William Laud, to impose strict High-Church reforms that earned him the most enemies among the English people, including Milton. Laud's programme of reform included a curbing of free-speech both in the press and in the pulpit in order to ensure religious uniformity within the Church of England. In addition to this, Laud angered a significant number within the Church by the emphasis he placed upon the ceremonial aspects of Christian worship, uncomfortably reminiscent to many Protestants of a Catholicism to which they were deeply opposed. Laud's measures were perceived by many as a subversion of Reformation principles because, in their eyes, uniting State and Church would result in a damaging confusion between political and religious liberty. As a result many Christians, especially the **Puritans**, felt driven out of the Church and a tide of religious persecution ensued. Milton himself wrote that 'tyranny had invaded the church' (*The Reason of Church Government*) and that Laud's reforms had effectively 'Church-outed' him against his own will (*ibid*).

Ultimately, it would be this atmosphere of non-toleration within the church that would motivate many otherwise moderate Anglicans, Milton among them, to become more Puritan in their religious sympathies. Laud's unpopular policies resulted in a backlash from Parliament, a flurry of petitioning and publishing against him, and his eventual execution. Even more seriously, Laud's policies backfired on Charles. Rather than furnishing the King with a loyal, united nation as they were designed to do, the reforms made him vulnerable to the charge of religious and political tyranny.

CHANGE IN POLITICAL MENTALITY

In Milton's lifetime, a significant shift had occurred in the imaginations of the English people. A new revolutionary spirit was expressed by those who opposed the King in that they emphasized the right of man to have a government that would be answerable to its own subjects. Blind loyalty towards tradition and custom had been decisively rejected by those who fought on the side of Parliament: they fought Charles's army for the freedom to hold to their own consciences in religious matters, for a Parliament that would be able to make its own laws, and for a Church free of the Episcopal structure that epitomized authoritarian rule.

Milton made it his life's work to defend the ideal of a political system led by virtuous, God-fearing men who would acknowledge that man's religious freedom should be left to the judgement of his own mind. Works such as *Areopagitica* and *The Tenure of Kings and Magistrates* promoted this ideal, by calling for freedom from religious intolerance and political tyranny.

CIVIL WAR: 1642–6

The first phase of the war raged from 1642 to 1645, with Charles seeking support from Ireland, and Parliament achieving backing from the Scots. Eventually Charles's Royalist army was defeated, largely thanks to a minority Parliamentary force, the **Independents**, who had formed what they called the New Model Army under the direction of Oliver Cromwell. Charles, his Royalist force finally overwhelmed by the New Model Army, surrendered himself to the Scots in May 1646 and brought the first phase of the Civil War to an end.

Although Parliament had been successful in defeating the Royalists, they were radically divided in their own religious and political sympathies. This split was between the **Presbyterians** in Parliament – who wanted to reappoint the King on the condition that the Church would follow a Presbyterian model – and the Independents – who favoured persevering with the hostilities until a settlement could be achieved that would guarantee religious freedom. The mainly Presbyterian Parliament proved themselves unequal to the task of reconciling religious dissension. As Milton observed dryly in a sonnet

> ## KEYWORD
>
> **Independent:** the Independents rejected the need for a State Church and believed instead that Protestant sects should co-exist in a spirit of mutual toleration and respect for each other's religious freedom.
>
> **Presbyterians:** the Presbyterians were distinguished from other Puritan movements by their belief that church government should be organized by a Synod of Presbyters, both on a local and national level.

of 1646 *On the new forcers of conscience*, 'New presbyter is but old priest writ large'. Although they had been rebelling against Laud's High-Anglican reforms of the Church, the Presbyterians were equally disdainful of rival Protestant sects and enforced a printing ordinance to censor all publications. Milton, whose second edition of the *Doctrine and Discipline of Divorce* had been published without a license, immediately sided with the Independents and began writing on the topic of religious freedom. In his *Areopagitica* (1644), Milton argued that 'Truth is strong, next to the Almighty. She needs no policies, nor stratagems, nor licensings to make her victorious.'

Parliament had thus failed to live up to the hopes of the Independents: it had not guaranteed religious freedom for the people of England.

CIVIL WAR: 1647–49
When, in 1647, Charles and the Scots reached an agreement in which the King promised to introduce Presbyterianism within the Church of England in return for Scottish military support, the war resumed in earnest. This second phase of the Civil War would be brief and bloody. Cromwell's New Model Army quickly overcame the Scots at Preston in August 1648 making Parliament once again victorious. The King's decision to align himself with the Scots had made it impossible for Cromwell to trust him; Charles was now viewed as a threat to the new Commonwealth and, once Cromwell had ensured that Parliament had rid itself of right-wing and moderate members who would disagree with the King's execution, he ordered Charles I's trial. The King was sentenced to death on 27 January 1649 and was beheaded three days later.

MILTON'S ROLE IN THE COMMONWEALTH GOVERNMENT (1649–60)
The execution of Charles I backfired badly upon Cromwell's new regime. Public memory of the King transformed him from a power-hungry, underhanded tyrant into a martyr figure. Cromwell badly needed an advocate both for the State's action in committing regicide, and for the legitimacy of the new regime. Milton gladly stepped in to

fill that role. Unsolicited, and only weeks after the King's death, he published *The Tenure of Kings and Magistrates* (1649), claiming that the right to rule is a privilege extended by the people to those who show themselves worthy of it. This sentiment would echo throughout Milton's later work, especially in *Paradise Lost* where it comes to classic statement in Abidel's speech to Satan:

> This is servitude,
> To serve the unwise, or him who hath rebelled
> Against his worthier, as thine now serve thee.
> Thyself not free, but to thyself enthralled
>   (VI. 177–81)

The unwise Charles, in Milton's opinion, had illegitimately ruled over those who were worthier than him. His misuse of power had enthralled the English people and, according to *The Tenure of Kings and Magistrates*, subjects should have the right to execute rulers who are guilty of such misuse. Upon publication of *The Tenure*, Cromwell offered Milton the post of Secretary for Foreign Languages in the new Commonwealth (see Biography).

Milton published frantically in his new role: writing *Eikonoklastes* (meaning image-breaker) in response to a book written by the King prior to his execution, and replying to Continental criticism of the Commonwealth's illegality in three *Defensio pro populo anglicano* (Defences of the English people). His emphasis was always upon the ideal of a political system ruled by virtuous men who would permit freedom of an individual's religious conscience. Milton was to be disappointed in the ability of the English to seize upon what he saw as their golden opportunity for freedom in the form of the Commonwealth. It was precisely this disappointment that motivated his poetic genius in *Paradise Lost*.

MILTON AT THE RESTORATION (1660–74)

Despite the best efforts of Milton to justify the ways of the government to its subjects, Cromwell's death in September 1658, leaving his son

Richard to succeed him, left England heading towards anarchy. In May 1660 the Stuart monarchy was restored to the throne in the shape of Charles II. A wave of Royalist sympathy swept through the country, soon to sink as the new King's incompetence and tyranny became apparent. Religious persecution began in earnest, with non-conformists finding themselves facing discrimination and penalties in the new regime.

Milton himself was arrested and briefly imprisoned for his defence of the regicide (see Biography). Evidence of his unswerving loyalty to the ideal of political and religious liberty in England was the fact that Milton published yet another anti-monarchical tract, *The Ready and Easy Way to Establish a Free Commonwealth*, only weeks before the inevitable Restoration. As it was, the occurrence of the Restoration meant that the great Commonwealth experiment to resolve the tension between political supremacy and religious freedom had failed the English people.

✳ ✳ ✳ SUMMARY ✳ ✳ ✳

● In the decades leading up to Milton's birth, England experienced radical social, religious and political changes with every change of monarch.

● In Milton's lifetime, religious tension and politcal dissatisfaction expressed itself in hostility towards Charles I. Those who opposed the King demanded a government which would be answerable to its own subjects.

● As a result of the English Civil War, a Commonwealth government was established under the leadership of Oliver Cromwell, and King Charles was executed.

● Milton supported the new regime, publishing many political tracts in defence of the Commonwealth state. After the Restoration of the monarchy in 1660, Milton was arrested and briefly imprisoned for his role in Cromwell's government.

4 Major Works 1: *Paradise Lost*

BACKGROUND TO *PARADISE LOST*

Paradise Lost, Milton's greatest poetic achievement, was conceived as early as 1639, when the poet was barely 30, and we also find references to it in the notebooks of 1640–1. The poem itself, however, did not begin to take real shape until around 1658–63. When it was published in 1667 by Samuel Simmons, Milton received only a £5 down payment (a hard bargain even in those days) and the promise of £5 to be paid once the balance of the first edition – 1,300 copies of the poem – had been sold.

An **epic** poem in ten books, *Paradise Lost* was later reorganized into 12 books for the edition of 1674. By this time, Milton had added an Argument to each book and a prose defence of his decision to write *Paradise Lost* in unrhymed blank verse. The poem's immediate reception was enthusiastic, with poet Andrew Marvell writing a verse tribute to it (added to the 1674 edition), and Sir John Denham praising *Paradise Lost* in the House of Commons.

> **KEYWORD**
>
> Epic: a long narrative poem written on a grand and serious subject, narrated in a lofty style, often incorporating battles, legends and the supernatural. Belonging to this genre (in Greek) is Homer's *Iliad* and (in Latin) Virgil's *Aeneid*.

Biographer A. N. Wilson writes that for all 1,300 copies to have sold out in the first two years of publication, '… it must have meant that almost every bookish or literary person in England had read or looked into *Paradise Lost* before 1669' (*The Life of John Milton*).

Milton, by now nearly at the end of his life, found his principal aim had been accomplished: England celebrated him, and would continue to celebrate him, as one of the finest poets she had ever produced.

PARADISE LOST AND GENESIS 1-3

Paradise Lost takes as its subject matter the grandest themes imaginable: the creation of human beings; the origin of evil; and the possibility of reconciliation between God and his rebellious creatures. Milton's aim in *Paradise Lost* is nothing less ambitious than to illuminate his readers' understanding of God, encouraging them to lift up their hearts and minds to worship their divine creator and liberator. At the very outset of his epic, Milton follows the convention of declaring to his readers the purpose of the poem and asking for aid in this enterprise:

> Of man's first disobedience and the fruit
> Of that forbidden tree, whose mortal taste
> Brought death into the world and all our woe,
> With loss of Eden, till one greater Man
> Restore us, and regain the blissful seat,
> Sing Heav'nly Muse ... (I: 1–6)

The sense of these lines, notoriously difficult to interpret on first reading (see Early critical approaches), can be gathered by taking the sixth line to read as the first, i.e. 'Sing Heav'nly Muse / Of man's first disobedience ...' and so on. On this reading, Milton asks his poetic **Muse** to recite to him the story of man's creation, disobedience and Fall. The 'greater Man' in the fourth line is Jesus Christ, who will make an appearance in Books III and XI of the poem as the one who can restore humanity's broken relationship with God. Having identified the poem as epic by summoning his Muse in the conventional manner, Milton goes on to characterize the work's distinctively Christian purpose by explaining that it is the Holy Spirit himself, a 'Heav'nly Muse', who must provide his inspiration.

KEYWORD

Muse: the Muses were the nine daughters of Zeus in classical Greek mythology, each of whom presided over one art form. It is traditional for an epic poet to appeal to a particular Muse to help him write his work.

Taking the narratives of the biblical book Genesis, chapters 1–3 as his starting point, Milton poetically recreates the famous story of Adam and Eve in the Garden of Eden. Too long to quote in full here, the following is an excerpt from the book of Genesis in which Satan, disguised as a snake, comes into paradise to tempt Eve to eat fruit from the tree of knowledge, knowing that God has forbidden her to do so:

> Now the serpent was more subtle than any other wild creatures that the LORD God had made. He said to the woman ... 'God knows that when you eat of ... (the fruit) your eyes will be opened, and you will be like God, knowing good and evil.' So when the woman saw that the tree was good for food, and that it was a delight to the eyes, and that the tree was to be desired to make one wise, she took of its fruit and ate; and she also gave some to her husband, and he ate.
>
> (Genesis 3: 1, 5–6, RSV)

Milton's rewriting of the Fall of humanity (known as such because it represents the original downward turn in human fortunes, the beginning of all evil and suffering) squeezes the biblical account to the full, and extends it into over 10,000 lines of poetry. In order to achieve such epic length and gravity while making a well-known story his own, Milton absorbs himself in dialogue with a range of supplementary material extraordinary in its scope, including classical allusion, philosophical speculation, contemporary political analysis, and theological debate. In this way, *Paradise Lost* engages with every significant aspect of human culture. Science, art, religion and politics are all invoked to back Milton's claim in *Paradise Lost* that '... without love no happiness' (VIII: 621). That is to say, on reading Milton's great epic the reader encounters much more than simply a poem, she is confronted with a call to turn back to loving God and her fellow human beings, a summons to regain that which her first parents, Adam and Eve, lost in their Fall from grace.

THE STRUCTURE OF *PARADISE LOST*

The Fall of Satan and the creation of hell (Books 1–11)

Book I

Milton opens the poem in Book I with a question to the Holy Spirit himself:

> ... say first what cause
> Moved our grand parents in that happy state,
> Favoured of Heav'n so highly, to fall off
> From their Creator, and transgress his will
> ... Who first seduced them to that foul revolt?

(I: 28–31, 33)

Following the example of Homer and Virgil who begin their epic poems by asking a Muse to tell them which gods had brought about the events of the story, Milton asks the Holy Spirit 'who first seduced' Adam and Eve to sin. His use of the epic opening question, however, represents far more than simple adherence to poetic convention. Milton is also taking the opportunity to pose a probing theological question that will continue to trouble him throughout *Paradise Lost*. If God is the uncaused cause of the universe, the first link in a chain of cause and effect beyond which there is no transcending, as theologians from medieval times onwards have reasoned, then what sort of cause can we ascribe to the Fall of mankind? The poet is swift to voice Genesis's answer to this question, 'Th' infernal Serpent; he it was' (l. 34). Milton's characterization of this serpent Satan and the 'companions of his fall' in Book I, though, is surprising in its ascription of **heroic** qualities. We are introduced to the arch enemy of humankind in this first book of the poem as he awakes troops of other fallen angels, rallies their

> **KEYWORD**
>
> Hero: neither entirely good nor entirely evil, Aristotle says that a good tragic hero should be a fusion of both. Traditionally, the tragic hero should be more honourable than we ourselves are, in order that his fall from happiness to misery – due to an error of judgement or a mistaken act – should move us to pity and fear.

morale, summons a council and arranges for his palace, Pandemonium, to be built.

Consider these lines, spoken by Satan as he surveys the hell to which he has fallen after an unsuccessful uprising against God and compares it to the heaven that he has just lost:

> ... Farewell happy fields
> Where joy for ever dwells: hail horrors, hail
> Infernal world, and thou profoundest hell
> Receive thy new possessor: one who brings
> A mind not to be changed by place or time.

(I: 249–53)

Satan's unflinching acknowledgement of the joy he has lost, and his willingness to greet and internalize the horror of hell – described elsewhere in the poem as a burning lake of fire – holds a powerful poetic fascination both for Milton and for his reader. This speech, running from lines 241–64, and an earlier monologue by Satan at lines 82–124, form the dramatic centre of the first book, leaving the reader unsure whether the rebel angel is the hero or the villain of the piece.

Book II

Book II of *Paradise Lost* falls into two interrelated parts. The first of these parts runs from lines 1–628 and concerns the council debates in hell between the devils as to what they should do next. One after another, the devils reason that they should either wage another assault on heaven, resign themselves to the hell into which they have been thrown, or attempt to sabotage God's recent creation of Earth 'the happy seat / Of some new race call'd Man' (ll. 347–8). In this section, Milton's emphasis is upon an unimpeded exchange of argument which would have been familiar to him from his experience as a public servant and political pamphleteer for Cromwell's government (see Biography). Many critics have even suggested links between the political rhetoric of the fallen angels and passages in Milton's various political tracts.

The second section of Book II, running from lines 629 to 1055, involves the decision of Satan's 'horrid crew' to adopt Beelzebub's suggestion. As a consequence, Satan decides to visit Earth in order to find a means to be revenged upon God. These lines follow the Devil's journey through hell to its gates – which are guarded by the personified figures of Sin and Death – and contain some of Milton's most startling and sublime poetry (see Why read Milton today?).

Paradise (Books III–VIII)

Book III

Milton's Argument to Book III, added before publication of the second edition, claims that in it:

> God … clears his own justice and wisdom from all imputation, having
> created man free and able enough to withstand his tempter.

Whether the reader agrees with Milton's assessment that God is 'cleared' from all responsibility for man's Fall, or whether she sees a discrepancy between the claims of Milton's Argument and the results of his poetry, will depend partly on her interpretation of certain ambiguous passages in the poem. For instance, at the very beginning of the third book, the blind poet addresses a prayer to God as his light:

> Hail holy Light, offspring of Heav'n first-born,
> Or of th'Eternal coeternal beam
> May I express thee unblamed?   (III: 1–3)

While invoking God's presence to enlighten his poetry, Milton still engages in an anxious self-examination. 'May I express thee unblamed?' may thus be read as either the orthodox theological question, Is it possible to express the reality of the transcendent God in human language without committing the sin of **idolatry**? or as the unorthodox, more unsettling question, Is it possible to write of God's part in the Fall of man without imputing any blame to Him?

KEYWORD

Idolatry: the worship of an image or representation of God rather than the worship of God himself.

In Book III of *Paradise Lost*, Milton attempts to do the incredible: to invent dramatic speeches for God, a dialogue between God the Father and God the Son, without writing a blasphemous fiction. Using what the Romantic poet Coleridge would later describe as 'the simplest and sternest language' with 'no poetic diction, no amplification, no pathos, no affection' (*Table Talk*, S. T. Coleridge, 4 September 1833), Milton describes God as observing Satan flying towards Earth, and foretelling his success in provoking Adam and Eve's Fall 'sufficient to have stood, yet free to fall' (l. 99).

In unadorned yet stunning poetry Jesus Christ, the Son of God, offers to substitute himself for man, undergoing the punishment that man should receive for his disobedience, 'Behold me then, me for him, life for life/ I offer, on me let thine anger fall; / Account me man ...' (ll. 236–8). His offer of ransom is accepted by the Father and the angels in heaven proclaim Christ the Saviour and sing praises to God. Meanwhile, Satan disguises himself as a cherub and deceives the angel Uriel into giving him the directions to Earth. With characteristic speed, Satan 'Throws his steep flight in many an airy wheel' (l. 741) and alights on the top of Mount Niphates in Armenia.

Book IV

Satan, having almost arrived at the Garden of Eden, falls into a fit of tortured self-doubt. In the 26-line sentence that opens the fourth book, Milton represents the psychological reality of Satan's decision to possess and internalize hell:

> ... and from the bottom stir
> The hell within him, for within him hell
> He brings, and round about him, nor from hell
> One step no more than from himself can fly
> By change of place ...

(IV: 19–23)

Milton's compulsive repetition of 'he', 'him' and 'himself', and his use of the phrase 'hell within him' coupled with its immediate inversion 'within him hell', actually mimics the obsessive workings of Satan's tormented mind. The horrors, jealousies, doubts and dejections that Satan undergoes at the beginning of Book IV have thus taken the form of recurring mental distress, inescapable by 'change of place'. This anguished psychological portrait of Milton's most ambiguous character both compels and repulses the sympathies of the reader, recalling us to William Empson's comment that *Paradise Lost* 'is not good in spite of but especially because of its moral confusions' (*Milton's God*, 1961).

At last, Satan bids goodbye to his fear and remorse, invoking evil to 'be thou my good' (l. 110). As he reaches paradise, both the devil and the reader see Adam and Eve for the first time. Again, Satan's amazement at the beauty of God's latest creation, woman and man, 'whom my thoughts pursue / With wonder, and could love' (ll. 362–3) touchingly reveals his own sense of loss. Nevertheless, the Devil is resolved to be revenged upon God and, when he overhears the happy pair discussing the Father's command not to eat from the Tree of Knowledge, he decides to use this knowledge to tempt Adam and Eve into disobedience.

As Satan is discovered by protecting angels squatting 'like a toad' (l. 800) at the ear of Eve, to tempt her in a dream with 'Vain hopes, vain aims, inordinate desires / Blown up with high conceits engend'ring pride' (ll. 808–9), he is brought to the archangel Gabriel and eventually flies back out of paradise.

Book V

As morning arrives and the pair awakes, Eve recounts to Adam her troubling dream:

Close at mine ear one called me forth to walk
With gentle voice, I thought it thine; it said,
'Why sleep'st thou Eve? now is the pleasant time,
The cool, the silent, save where silence yields
To the night-warbling bird …'

(V, ll.36–40)

Milton creates a palpably sexual charge to this passage by taking Satan's voice close to Eve's ear and allowing her to mistakenly attribute its gentleness to the voice of her husband. The predominance of 'l' alliteration in Satan's language slows the speech down, giving it a languid mood, while his sensual justification of the night's excellence tempts Eve to leave Adam's side and walk with the Devil to the Tree of Knowledge where he enjoins her to taste its forbidden fruit.

Adam's immediate reaction to her narrative, 'This uncouth dream, of evil sprung I fear; / Yet evil whence?' (ll. 98–9), reveals his anxiety to uncover the source of Eve's mental corruption. This anxiety, in turn, resonates with a puzzle which has prompted theologians of every generation to scratch their heads. That is, if evil can be said to have existed even as a possibility prior to the Fall of humanity, as this passage suggests, then how may we attribute its origin to anyone else but God, the creator of all things? Adam comforts Eve (and himself) with the notion that 'Evil into the mind of god or man / May come and go … and leave / No spot or blame behind …'(ll. 117–19); yet a certain disquiet is left in the mind of the reader as to how this evil may have come into the world in the first place.

It is this disquiet that Milton attempts to address by placing here, at the heart of the poem, a story entirely foreign to the source narratives of Genesis: the visit of the archangel Raphael to the Garden of Eden. In a dialogue that will last from the latter part of Book V through to Book VIII, Raphael is sent to paradise as God's chief minister in order to advise Adam and Eve of their duties and to warn them against the evils of disobedience. By adding this story to the biblical account, Milton hopes to demonstrate that God did everything possible to stop Adam and Eve from using their freedom unwisely.

As Raphael comes to Adam and Eve in the garden of Eden he is met with a show of friendly hospitality. The three enjoy a meal together, made by Eve and depicted by Milton in mouth-watering poetry, 'from sweet kernels pressed / She tempers dulcet creams …' (ll. 346–7). After dinner, prompted by Adam, the conversation turns to spiritual matters and Raphael explains many mysteries to him, including predestination, free will and the pre-history of man in which Satan rebelled against God and gathered a force of other dissident angels to go into battle against Him.

Book VI

In Book VI, Raphael continues to describe Satan's battle with God. Although Eve often withdraws from the conversation, she is kept up-to-date with the dialogue by Adam. On the third day of battle, Raphael relates, God sent his Son, Jesus Christ, to gain victory over Satan's forces. Riding in a chariot '… in his right hand / Grasping ten thousand thunders' (ll.835–6), the Son drove his enemies to the edge of heaven where, astonished and humiliated, they fell to their eternal punishment in hell.

Raphael's narration of Christ's victory over Satan is crucial to the poem because it reveals Milton's main aim in *Paradise Lost*, to persuade his readers of God's ultimate opposition to, and power over, evil. In the poem, the Son's triumph over the Devil occurs on the third day of battle in order that the average seventeenth-century reader, well-versed in the Scriptures, would be reminded of Christianity's ultimate answer to the problem of evil, **redemption** by faith in the Son of God who arose from death on the third day. Even before Adam and Eve have fallen, therefore, Milton is asking his readers to take comfort in a saviour who can defeat not only the character of Satan, but also death itself.

KEYWORD

Redemption: Deliverance from a state of slavery. In theology, the term is used to denote Christ's deliverance of humankind from sin.

At the close of Book VI, however, Raphael fulfils his mission from God and sternly warns Adam to avoid the devil's temptations:

> ... let it profit thee to have heard
> By terrible example the reward
> Of disobedience; firm they might have stood,
> Yet fell; remember, and fear to transgress.   (ll. 909–12)

Book VII

After calling once again upon his Muse, Milton appeals for inspiration to continue the poem and alludes to his own precarious public standing as an outspoken proponent of the Cromwellian cause, 'On evil days though fall'n, and evil tongues; / In darkness, and with dangers compassed round,' (ll. 26–7). Probably written after the Restoration of Charles II to the throne, many critics believe these lines imply the – now blind – poet's desolation at the failure of his hopes for an English Republic (see Historical, political and religious contexts).

The real theme of Book VII, though, is humankind's unquenchable thirst for knowledge in a world which seems to set strict limits on understanding. Still conversing with Raphael, Adam asks the archangel to reveal the great secrets of the universe, especially how and why God made it the way he did:

> ... if unforbid thou may'st unfold
> What we, not to explore the secrets ask
> Of his eternal empire, but the more
> To magnify his works, the more we know.   (ll. 94–97)

The theory of knowledge which Milton advances in *Paradise Lost* is not, as some critics suggest, merely a negative one. Instead, the poet makes it clear that although there are many secrets in the universe that it is not within man's capacity to understand, being truly human involves an entirely blameless desire to comprehend the cosmos in order to render praise to its creator.

Setting the scene for Book IX, in which Adam and Eve will disobey God's command by eating from the Tree of Knowledge, Milton draws the analogy between humanity's appetite for knowledge and our appetite for food. Both appetites, according to the archangel, must be enjoyed in moderation in order to avoid physical or intellectual sickness. Despite this warning, Raphael accedes to Adam's request and relates to him how God decided to create the world in six days through his Son.

Book VIII

Still conversing with Raphael, Adam inquires about the movement of the planets, especially concerning the position of the Earth in relation to the other heavenly spheres. It should be remembered that when Milton wrote *Paradise Lost*, the **cosmological** debate over whether the Earth is the centre of the universe (the

> **KEYWORD**
>
> Cosmology: that branch of science which deals with the origin and structure of the universe.

Ptolemaic system), or whether the Earth revolves around the sun (the Copernican system) was at its most intense. More important than the decision Milton makes to follow one model or another – he refuses to reach any clear verdict on the matter – is Raphael's repeated declaration that humankind should:

> Solicit not thy thoughts with matters hid,
> Leave them to God above, him serve and fear ...   (ll. 167–8)

Human reason, according to Raphael, should not be employed in attempting to understand everything about the universe, as God keeps many 'matters hid' from our knowledge.

Adam recalls his own creation and his first discussion with God, including the divine command not to touch the fruit from the Tree of Knowledge. Pleading for a companion to share in the paradise which he inhabits, Adam recounts how he was first required to engage in intellectual debate with God. In a process rather similar to that to which Milton subjects his readers in *Paradise Lost*, Adam is guided by God through a discussion about the nature of his solitude, his desire for intelligent fellowship and, finally, the necessity of an equal partner in order to procreate. In this way, the first man is forced to articulate his objections and desires so that he might learn from them, just as Milton's reader is asked to explore her own intellectual problems with the Christian God in the hope that she might eventually overcome them.

Having taught Adam the value of right reason, God grants him his wish for a companion and creates Eve from Adam's rib. Following a moving account of his first meeting with the newly-created Eve, 'I waked / To find her, or for ever to deplore / Her loss' (ll. 478–80), Adam goes on to hint at the innocent sexual passion of their wedding night. After warning him about the importance of moderating one's sexual appetite, Raphael exhorts Adam to 'Be strong, live happy, and love, but first of all / Him whom to love is to obey, and keep / His great command' (ll .633–5). The two then part, and Raphael returns to heaven.

The temptation and Fall of Adam and Eve (Books IX–X)

Book IX
Mankind's Fall in Book IX from innocence to evil marks the climactic moment of *Paradise Lost*. Milton pictures Satan scoping the Earth and entering, appropriately, into the body of a sleeping serpent. Finding Eve alone at her work, Satan marvels at her innocence and beauty for a few last, terrible moments before he confirms himself in evil, 'Save what is in destroying, other joy / To me is lost.' (ll. 478-–9).

Following Adam's council with God, and Raphael's reasoning with the first pair, Milton once again makes dialogue the crucial element in the dramatic movement of this scene. The rhetorical devices of persuasion, argument, flattery, soothing and questioning are all employed by the Devil-turned-serpent in order to tempt Eve into disobeying the command of God. Satan tempts Eve physically, telling the mother of mankind that the forbidden fruit had:

> ... more pleased my sense
> Than smell of sweetest fennel, or the teats
> Of ewe or goat dropping with milk at ev'n ...   (ll. 580–2)

Appealing here to the senses of sight, smell, touch and taste (and doing so in poetry which delights the ear) the serpent hopes to seduce Eve into eating the fruit by comparing it to more wholesome pleasures. More significantly, though, the disguised Devil appeals to Eve's intellectual judgement in the hope of convincing her of the irrationality of God's command. Why, Satan asks in Book IX, should God want to forbid mankind from touching the fruit of the Tree of Knowledge? Is it because he wants keep humanity down? If so, why did he encase knowledge of good and evil into the Tree at creation? Indeed, the questions that Satan puts to Eve in this, the most important dialogue of the poem, are the very questions that a sensitive reader will have been asking herself throughout her reading of the poem:

> ... if what is evil
> Be real, why not known, since easier shunned?'   (ll. 698–9)

> 'Why then was this forbid? Why but to awe,
> Why but to keep ye low and ignorant,
> His worshippers ...   (ll7 03–5)

> ... can envy dwell
> In heav'nly breasts?   (ll. 729–30)

That is to say, if the Devil's arguments and questions are convincing to Eve, they are just as convincing to the reader of *Paradise Lost*. Simple condemnation of Eve as the originator of the Fall is thus rendered impossible by Milton. Instead, the reader is forced to recognize herself as implicated in the Fall of mankind, intellectually tempted in the present to agree with Satan's arguments at the crucial moment in human history. Eve, predictably, eats and reluctantly reports what has happened to Adam, bringing him some of the fruit to try. Her husband, realizing that she is condemned, decides to join her:

> ... if death
> Consort with thee, death is to me as life;
> So forcible within my heart I feel
> The bond of nature draw me to my own ...   (ll. 953–6)

Adam, keen that not even death should consort with Eve alone, jealously eats the fruit. Following a period of intense exhilaration and sexual pleasure the two suddenly realize their own nakedness, '... innocence, that as a veil / Had shadowed them from knowing ill, was gone ...' (ll. 1054–5). Just as Satan had promised, Adam and Eve are shown to have gained knowledge of good and evil but, in a cruel twist, their new understanding is shown to be knowledge of the good they have lost and the evil they have embraced.

'(D)estitute and bare / Of all their virtue' (ll. 1062–3), the pair cover their nakedness and, as they do so, the poet ends the book with a painful beginning. In the last line of Book IX, writing of Adam and Eve's deterioration into mutual recrimination 'And of their vain contést appeared no end' (l. 1189), Milton reveals that humanity's new life of fearful opposition to God will be one of perpetual strife. From this point forward, the tone of *Paradise Lost* changes as Adam and Eve confront their new destiny; no longer is Milton's poetry infused with the delight of humanity's pre-Fall innocence, rather the poem looks backwards wistfully to that which has been lost, and fearfully to that which is to come.

Book X

Observing Adam and Eve's act of defiance, God sends his Son to paradise to judge the offending couple. Hiding away in the trees from the sound of his voice, they eventually come forward to meet him with 'apparent guilt, / And shame, and perturbation and despair' (ll. 112–3). After they have confessed, though postponing the death sentence, Christ inflicts on the pair the prospect of a life limited by death, and encumbered with conflict, pain, oppression and back-breaking labour. On Satan, Christ pronounces a curse which will become crucial for an understanding of Book XII: that Eve's 'seed' (or offspring) 'shall bruise thy head, thou bruise his heel'(l. 181).

The abstract figures of Sin and Death, pictured by Milton as seated by the gates of hell, somehow smell out humanity's disobedience and, 'lured / With scent of living carcasses designed / For death ...' (ll. 276–8), they decide together to enter into paradise in order to feed upon Adam and Eve's unhappiness. As Satan returns to hell to proclaim his conquest, God inflicts a punishment to fit his crime against mankind by temporarily transforming him and his followers back into serpents.

While the angels in heaven rejoice at God's future triumph over Sin, Death and the Devil, Adam stands in misery on Earth, considering suicide but fearing the consequences:

> Yet one doubt
> Pursues me still, lest all I cannot die,
> ... I shall die a living death? O thought
> Horrid, if true! ...
>
> Can he make deathless death?   (ll. 782–3; 788–9; 798)

In his long and tormented **soliloquy**, Adam is made to repeat the words 'die' and 'death' over and again, his fallen reason moving in ever-decreasing circles to determine whether endless death would be preferable to a life plagued by suffering. The father of mankind remains plagued by these obsessive repetitions and unanswerable questions until Eve arrives. Although initially blaming her for their Fall, Adam quickly recovers the use of his reason and convinces Eve of God's grace towards mankind. In contrast to the attitude of proud, self-seeking

KEYWORD

Soliloquy: from the Latin *solus* 'alone' and *loqui* 'to speak', a soliloquy is a speech, often extensive in length, uttered by a character who is alone on the stage. In drama and dramatic poetry, the soliloquy allows a writer the opportunity to convey a character's inmost thoughts, feelings and motivations.

animosity described at the end of Book IX, the book ends with the couple kneeling in humble and repentant prayer 'with their sighs the air / Frequenting, sent from hearts contrite, in sign / Of sorrow unfeigned, and humiliation meek.' (ll. 1102–4).

Expulsion from paradise (Books XI–XII)

Book XI

The Son, seeing Adam and Eve's penitent and sorrowful state, intercedes with the Father on their behalf. God accepts Christ's intercession but decrees that the pair must leave Eden and never return; he sends the archangel Michael to dispossess them of their paradise and convey them out into the world. As Christopher Ricks has commented on *Paradise Lost*, '... of all

> **KEYWORD**
>
> Oxymoron: a figure of speech which combines incongruous and apparently contradictory words and meanings for a special effect.

Milton's touching **oxymorons**, perhaps the greatest is the title of his epic' (*Milton's Grand Style*, London, 1963).

As Michael comes to remove the transgressing couple, Eve laments the loss of Eden while Adam, after pleading with the archangel, quickly submits, realizing that to appeal against God's commands 'No more avails than breath against the wind, / Blown stifling back on him that breathes it forth' (ll. 311–13). Milton does not make clear whether this bleak summary of the situation – implying that God acts in the world as an impersonal and ruthless force, a 'wind' – is his own as well as Adam's. Instead, the reader is left to decide for herself how much God hears the prayers of human beings and how much his will is fixed in advance.

Michael reassures Adam that, although they will no longer dwell in paradise, God is present in all places and at all times: his grace will accompany the human pair wherever they go. Leading Adam to the top of a hill, the archangel then reveals to him the repercussions of his original sin on the future of mankind, inviting him to behold the effect of his crime on those, '… who never touched / Th'excepted tree, nor with the snake conspired, / Nor sinned thy sin, yet from thy sin derive / Corruption to bring forth more violent deeds.' (ll.425–8)

Emphasizing the passivity of Adam's successors – they are said to have 'never touched', 'nor … conspired', 'nor sinned' – Milton goes on to describe a doctrine of original sin whereby human beings biologically inherit moral corruption (and therefore moral responsibility) from the parents of mankind. Again, it is not clear how far Milton agrees with orthodox Christian doctrine on this point, and how far he regards the effects of sin ('… all maladies / Of ghastly spasm, or racking torture, qualms / Of heart-sick agony' ll. 481–2) to be God's responsibility, not man's. Refusing any simple answers, the poet instead places the spectre of human suffering before us, maintaining that mental and physical sickness, with the inevitable pain that attends it, will always pursue humanity in this life.

Showing Adam the history of man narrated in Genesis up to the point of the Flood, Michael first entreats Adam, 'Nor love thy life, nor hate; but what thou liv'st / Live well …' (ll. 553–4).

Book XII
The archangel Michael continues to relate to Adam the history of the Old Testament: the building of Babylon and the tower of Babel, the history of Abraham and his sons, the Israelites' journey to Egypt and their return to the Promised Land, and the chronicles of Moses and David. More important than all this, though, is Michael's description in lines 348–465 of the expected Saviour, the 'seed' of Eve promised in Book X. Referring to the coming Messiah, the Son of God, Michael recounts to Adam the New Testament reports of his incarnation, crucifixion, resurrection, and ascension, claiming that Christ's resurrection from the dead is the act that 'Shall bruise the head of Satan, crush his strength' (l. 430).

Adam responds to this news by contemplating whether he should be unhappy or overjoyed about his original Fall into sin:

> Full of doubt I stand,
> Whether I should repent me now of sin
> By me done and occasioned, or rejoice
> Much more, that much more good thereof shall spring,
> To God more glory, more good will to men
> From God, and over wrath grace shall abound.   (ll. 473–8)

Adam's sentiment, known theologically as the concept of the Fortunate Fall, is the belief that man receives more grace and good from God as a result of his Fall than he would have experienced if he had remained obedient. Milton's articulation of this Christian conviction is echoed in his later theological treatise, *Christian Doctrine*, where he writes that, in salvation, '… man, being delivered from sin and death … is raised to a far more excellent state of grace and glory than that from which he had fallen.' (*CD*, I, xiv). Also known as the *felix culpa* (Latin for *happy fault*), the paradox of the Fortunate Fall simply formalizes the insight that goodness is a relative term; paradoxically, human beings can truly understand the good only if they also come to a knowledge of evil.

Michael ends his instruction of Adam both positively – by promising that the gift of the Holy Spirit will live in the hearts of future believers 'the law of faith / Working through love, upon their hearts shall write, / To guide them in all truth …' (ll. 488–90) – and negatively – alerting him to the corruption of the future Christian Church.

Eve, previously asleep and oblivious to these revelations, now awakes and tells her husband of a dream sent by God to signify 'some great good'(l. 612). This dream, in many ways the saving counterpart to the dream of temptation described in Book V, leaves Eve determined to obey God's righteous judgement. Looking behind them at the paradise they have lost, the pair allow themselves to be led slowly from the Garden. In the last distressing lines of the poem Milton writes of the father and mother of mankind:

The world was all before them, where to choose
Their place of rest, and Providence their guide:
They hand in hand with wand'ring steps and slow,
Through Eden took their solitary way.   (ll. 646–9)

Milton ends his epic by recalling the reader to Adam and Eve's former innocence where '... hand in hand they passed, the loveliest pair / That ever since in love's embraces met' (IV ll. 321–2). The poem thus finishes with a companionship, but one that has been forever altered; the couple, though still together, will always remain essentially 'solitary'. In characteristically ambivalent fashion, Milton pictures Adam and Eve as both free, able to 'choose / Their place of rest', and as 'guided' by Providence. Their entry into the world at the close of *Paradise Lost* is thus both an ending and a beginning, marking as it does the distortion of humanity's relationships yet representing, too, the genesis of mankind's salvation.

---

* * *SUMMARY* * *

- *Paradise Lost* is an epic poem in 12 books, narrating the creation, temptation and Fall of Adam and Eve, and their expulsion from the garden of Eden.

- In it, Milton engages not only with the biblical narratives, but also with classical literature, philosophy, politics and contemporary theological debate.

- The poem gives an account of human freedom as an explanation of the existence of evil.

---

5 Major Works II: *Samson Agonistes*

BACKGROUND TO *SAMSON AGONISTES*

In 1671, following the collapse of the Commonwealth and the Restoration of the monarchy, Milton published a volume containing his last two great poems: *Paradise Regained* and *Samson Agonistes* (Samson the Champion, or Wrestler). The debate about when *Samson* was written is ongoing in contemporary criticism, with many favouring a traditional dating of 1666–70 but some, notably W. R. Parker in his biography of Milton (1968), arguing for a date as early as 1647.

Taking a passage from the biblical book of Judges as its theme, *Samson Agonistes* tells the story of Samson's imprisonment at the hands of the Philistines, his struggle to come to terms with his fallen state and his courage in enduring the fate that God has ordained for him. Although self-consciously a dramatic poem, *Samson* was probably not intended for performance upon the stage. Instead, Milton's introspective concentration on one character and his fate in *Samson Agonistes* lends itself more easily to private reading.

Despite the biblical provenance of the story, *Samson* has often been compared to the classical Greek tragedies, especially *Prometheus Bound* by Aeschylus and *Oedipus at Colonus* by Sophocles. Yet, unlike *Paradise Lost*, *Samson Agonistes* avoids direct reference to classical literature and maintains instead the original simplicity and power of the Old Testament narrative. For this reason many critics argue that, despite its Greek structure, the poem is more Hebraic and Christian than Hellenic in spirit. Although written mainly in blank verse, the **metrical** arrangement of *Samson* is highly original, and rhyming lines are scattered unpredictably throughout. Unity of time, place and action are all preserved.

> **KEYWORD**
>
> Meter: from the Greek for *measure*, meter refers to the regular pattern of beats, the rhythmical variation of stressed and unstressed syllables, in poetry.

Although it is tempting to read the poem as a thinly disguised piece of autobiography (revolving around a blind hero whose political ambitions have failed), it should be born in mind that *Samson* may have been written long before Milton's own political disappointments. More important than its reference to the poet's life and time is its relevance to our own. In his prose introduction to the poem, Milton writes

KEYWORD

Homoeopathic: a branch of medicine in which patients are given small doses of salts or drugs which would, in a healthy person, cause symptoms of the disease itself.

that tragedy should actually change its readers, 'raising pity and fear, or terror, to purge the mind of those and such-like passions'. This **homoeopathic** theory of tragedy, first put forward by the ancient Greek thinker Aristotle, emphasizes the importance of a reader's personal experience of the poem. By taking part in Samson's misfortunes, Milton implies, the reader should become mentally empowered to confront the suffering and pain in her own life, reducing such negative emotions 'to just measure with a kind of delight, stirred up by reading or seeing those passions well imitated'.

THE STRUCTURE OF *SAMSON AGONISTES*

The poem opens as Samson, a Jewish military hero made blind and captive by the Philistines, pathetically staggers towards a shady place where he can rest from his prison labour. On a day set aside for a festival in honour of the Philistines' sea-god Dagon, Samson laments his newly wretched state of captivity 'Ask for this great deliverer now, and find him / Eyeless in Gaza at the mill with slaves' (ll. 40–1). In this opening soliloquy (see Glossary) Samson reveals that his troubles began when he divulged the secret of his superhuman strength (the length of his hair!) to his wife Dalila, a Philistine who betrayed him to her people. As the poem continues, the hero is interrupted by friends from his tribe, the Chorus, who attempt unsuccessfully to comfort him.

Samson's father Manoa is the next character to arrive on the scene. Appalled by his son's condition and questioning divine providence, 'I prayed for children ... / Who would be now a father in my stead?'

(ll. 352, 355), Manoa unfolds his plan to pay a ransom to the Philistines in return for his son's release. Samson, however, insists that his punishment is fully deserved; he rebukes himself for telling Dalila the secret source of his God-given strength and prays that his life will end quickly.

Dalila, 'bedecked, ornate, and gay, / … Like a stately ship' (ll. 712, 714), sails into the poem and begs her husband for forgiveness, promising him a life of ease and comfort. Turning her away contemptuously, Samson compares his estranged wife to a hyena, 'the only animal that digs up graves to get at the bodies of the dead' (*Milton: Complete Shorter Poems*, John Carey, 1968, n. 748 p. 369).

Following his exchanges with Manoa and Dalila, having become more confident in his remaining mental and physical strength, Samson is visited by the 'giant Harapha' (l. 1068), a Philistinian strong man. Bating the champion with gibes against God, Harapha is quickly challenged by Samson; in a moment of keen insight, the hero anticipates the calamitous ending of the poem by threatening to '… lay thy structure low, / Or swing thee in the air, then dash thee down / To the hazard of thy brains and shattered sides' (ll. 1239–41). The Chorus gleefully announces Harapha's departure from the scene, 'His giantship is gone somewhat crestfall'n' (l. 1244).

At last, an officer of state arrives to demand that Samson appear publicly before the Philistines to perform feats of strength during their festival to Dagon. After refusing once, the hero privately deliberates and decides to leave with the officer. Soon a messenger arrives and relates how Samson pulled down the two supporting pillars of the building in which the Philistines were assembled to watch him, killing everyone including himself. The poem ends with the Chorus announcing that all has turned out for the best.

SAMSON AS A TYPE OF CHRIST

In *Samson Agonistes*, Milton follows the Medieval and Renaissance tradition of depicting Samson as a type of Christ, a humble figure who alone can bring salvation to his people.

... I a prisoner chained, scarce freely draw
The air imprisoned also, close and damp,
Unwholesome draught: but here I feel amends,
The breath of heaven fresh blowing, pure and sweet,
With day-spring born; here leave me to respire.

(Samson Agonistes, ll. 7–11)

Reversing the movement of *Paradise Lost* – where a free woman and man bring alienation to the rest of humanity – Samson is depicted as a prisoner who brings liberty to his nation. Even though the hero is devoid of even basic human pleasures, his enthusiasm for being outside again in the 'breath of heaven fresh blowing' demonstrates a dynamic stasis like that of Christ in *Paradise Regained* (see Major themes), an unquestioning trust in the goodness of God. Yet something more profound is also being suggested here. In his description of the wind as the 'breath of heaven', in contrast to the 'unwholesome draught' of prison air, Samson is made to allude to a passage in the New Testament where the writer asserts that 'All scripture is God-breathed, and is profitable for doctrine, for reproof, for correction, for instruction in righteousness' (2 Tim 3:16, *KJV*). The breath of heaven blowing upon Samson is thus made to correspond to the voice of God in the Bible, the revelation of God to man.

THE NATURAL LAW AND THE MORAL LAW

In 1651, Thomas Hobbes wrote a momentous treatise on political philosophy, *Leviathan*, in which he overturned received Christian ideas about humanity's innate moral instincts, maintaining instead that man is an entirely sordid creature, acting only out of self-interest and self-love. Hobbes's famous statements in *Leviathan* that the life of man in this state of nature is 'solitary, poore, nasty, brutish and short', in which 'the notions of Right and Wrong, Justice and Injustice, have ... no place', would lead to his construction of a political philosophy in which the State is given the power to punish those who act against the peace, or 'Law of Nature'. For Hobbes, it is thus human selfishness, and not obedience to a moral law commanded by God, which has become the fundamental element for an understanding of human motivation.

Milton, by contrast, attempts to demonstrate in *Samson Agonistes* that human beings were created to trust and obey a divine judge:

> Yet stay, let me not rashly call in doubt
> Divine prediction; ...
> Whom have I to complain of but myself?
> ...
>
> But peace, I must not quarrel with the will
> Of highest dispensation, which herein
> Haply had ends above my reach to know ...   (SA, ll. 43–6; 60–3)

Although Samson remains blind and in captivity, a situation similar to that which would confront Milton himself in later life (see Biography), he reaches a moment of insight in which he realizes that the moral law of God is beyond his mortal understanding. God's 'highest dispensation', for Samson, is not ultimately open to question (questions abound in this poem) but must be submitted to willingly; as the prophet Isaiah writes in the Old Testament, 'For my thoughts are not your thoughts, neither are your ways my ways, says the LORD. (Isaiah 55:8)' In his determination to 'not rashly call in doubt / Divine prediction', Samson is indirectly – and favourably – compared with Eve in *Paradise Lost* who plucks the forbidden fruit of knowledge with a 'rash hand' (IX, l. 780). Milton presents Samson as a man who has come to trust in God *despite* his appalling living conditions; his liberty is not constituted in the freedom to act in the way he desires, as in Hobbes's *Leviathan*, but in the freedom to have relationship with an absolutely good (if sometimes incomprehensible) God.

PROVIDENCE OR FATE?

Samson Agonistes, like *Paradise Lost*, is intimately concerned with the justice of God in inflicting pain and suffering on mankind. Unlike Adam and Eve in *Paradise Lost*, though, Samson – like us – has been born into a world that is already fallen and corrupted. A strong sense of tragic fatalism is present throughout the poem in a way that is at odds with its ostensibly Christian message of salvation. For example, despite the Chorus's attempts to comfort the now decrepit champion with the notion of divine **providence**, it is difficult to escape Northrop Frye's impression of them, 'standing around uttering timid complacencies in teeth loosening doggerel'.

In particular the Chorus's claim at the end of the poem (after the destruction of the temple and all of the people inside it) that 'All is best' (l.1745) does not do justice to the reader's feeling of moral outrage at the act of violence perpetrated by its hero. As Joan S. Bennett writes:

> Teachers have observed how very differently the drama is experienced by Jewish students whose relatives faced the Holocaust and by Palestinian students who live in Israeli-occupied territories, as each set of readers deals with a tendency toward literal identification with the Hebrew or Philistine side of Milton's biblical source.
>
> ('Reading *Samson Agonistes*', *The Cambridge Companion to John Milton*, ed. Dennis Richard Danielson, 1989)

In this way, *Samson Agonistes* generates many opposing interpretations. Whether its world-view is that of the ancient Greeks – that is, profoundly fatalistic in spirit – or whether its message is one of Judeo-Christian hope, is never finally resolved by Milton.

✳ ✳ ✳ SUMMARY ✳ ✳ ✳

- *Samson Agonistes* retells the biblical story of Samson's imprisonment and slavery to the Philistines.

- Critics debate whether the poem is more Hebraic and Christian or Hellenic in character.

- Milton believed that *Samson Agonistes*, like all great tragedy, should actually change its readers for the better.

6 Major Themes

For Milton, no expression in his poetry is merely ornamental, each word earns its place in the larger design. For this reason, it is important to develop a sensitivity to the techniques and sounds of poetry in order to understand and take pleasure in Milton's artistry. As Wolfgang Iser writes in *The Art of Reading* (1976), 'The reader's enjoyment begins when he himself becomes productive, i.e., when the text allows him to bring his own faculties into play'.

ACTION AND INACTION

Throughout *Paradise Lost*, Milton describes humanity's alienation from God in traditional Christian terms as a Fall into a state of God-forgetfulness and disobedience. This **metaphor** – which alludes to man's bodily activity as a symbol of his spiritual activity – is extended throughout the poetry (and particularly *Paradise Lost*) to offer us tantalizing insights into Milton's theology. Whether the characters in his poems are standing, stooping, kneeling, falling, walking or sitting is never a matter of

indifference to the poet; indeed, it is often possible to chart a character's spiritual decline or progress in Milton's poetry simply in terms of their physical posture.

The character of Satan in *Paradise Lost*, at once alluring and repellent, can be seen as an heir to the heroes of Renaissance tragedy, especially to the character of Faustus in Christopher Marlowe's *Dr Faustus* (1604). Marlowe's play recounts the legend of a man, Faustus, who surrenders his soul in return for 24 years of life in which the Devil must give him whatever his lust for knowledge, power, wealth or sex will command. As Faustus's body lies torn to pieces by devilish spirits at the very close of the play, the chorus leaves us with a bleak moral:

> Faustus is gone. Regard his hellish fall,
> Whose fiendful fortune may exhort the wise
> Only to wonder at unlawful things,
> Whose deepness doth entice such forward wits,
> To practice more than heavenly power permits.   (V, iii, ll. 24–8)

Just as Faustus lies fallen because he transgressed divine command, so Satan in *Paradise Lost* is seen to over-reach the permitted bounds of knowledge and power set by God; his hellish fall is depicted as the punishment for transporting himself over and above God's laws. Although the sins of Milton's Devil are spiritual – pride, envy and lawless ambition – the progression of his evil in the poem, like that in *Dr Faustus*, is characterized physically:

> ... lifted up so high
> I sdained subjection, and thought one step higher
> Would set me highest
>
> ...
>
> O had his powerful destiny ordained
> Me some inferior angel, I had stood
> Then happy; no unbounded hope had raised
> Ambition ...'   (*PL*, IV, ll.49–51, 58–61)

Satan's evil, his disdain of subjection to divine government and his desire to challenge God's sovereignty, is reflected in the poetry as a desire for physical appropriation. Note Satan's use of passive and active physical metaphors to narrate his spiritual state: this great anti-hero of Milton's epic describes himself as inertly 'lifted' by God before his rebellion but dynamically taking 'one step higher' in his attempt to overthrow divine rule. This transgression is reflected in the line 'I (di)*sdained* subjection, and thought one step higher', by an additional metrical beat, the word 'higher' literally oversteps the **blank verse** construction of the poem and thus enacts Satan's gesture of over-reaching ambition. Although these physical and verbal challenges to God's authority are an extraordinary testimony to the agency of free will – so attractive to the reader that William Blake would later accuse Milton of being 'of the Devil's party without knowing it' – the poet also provides verbal cues to recognize and condemn Satan's evil. The **sibilance** of 'so ... sdained subjection ... step ... set' suggest serpent-like slitheriness, while the auditory ambivalence of 'sdained', meaning 'disdained' but sounding as 'stained' will return to haunt us later in *Paradise Lost* when Adam laments that his Fall has left him 'now soiled and stained' (IX, l. 1076).

> **KEYWORDS**
>
> **Blank verse:** this verse form consists of unrhymed lines, ten beats long, usually in iambic meter. Closest to the natural cadences of English speech, blank verse is the most widely-used of verse forms in English poetry and drama.
>
> **Sibilance:** an alliterative repetition and playing upon the letter 's', usually at the beginning of words or stressed syllables in poetry.

KNOWLEDGE

The activity which Milton reserves for special condemnation in *Paradise Lost*, the mental movement of rebellion which determines all subsequent evil in the poem, is the desire for God-like knowledge. As the poet Lord Byron would later lament:

> Sorrow is knowledge: they who know the most
> Must mourn the deepest o'er the fatal truth,
> The Tree of Knowledge is not that of Life.   (*Manfred*, I,I, ll. 9–11)

This recognition of the fatal truth that acquisition of forbidden knowledge is the death of innocence rather than the birth of a new, rich life, was originally Milton's insight. In Book IV of *Paradise Lost*, the poet describes Adam and Eve sleeping in their perfect pre-Fall state:

> These lulled by nightingales embracing slept,
> And on their naked limbs the flow'ry roof
> Show'red roses, which the morn repaired. Sleep on,

> Blest pair; and O yet happiest if ye seek
> No happier state, and know to know no more.   (IV, ll. 771–5)

The first man and woman are lovingly depicted by Milton as perfectly prone: lulled, sleeping and naked. Using erotic imagery, with a shower of roses falling upon the naked figures of Adam and Eve, the poet invites appreciation of a wonderfully loving stasis. The couple are invited to '[s]leep on', beautifully and innocently still. By his daring juxtaposition of the words 'know' and 'no' four times in the last line quoted, Milton reminds us that the act of obedience required by God is paradoxical, most animated by stillness and most spiritually observant in when involved in submission. This is not to say that Milton advocates human passivity as a means of achieving spirituality, rather he is suggesting that the action of obedience to God involves a willing relinquishment of our pride and ambition, and an enthusiastic abandonment of our doubtful questioning.

DISCOVERY AS FORM

In his dramatization of man's inner life in *Paradise Lost*, Milton is careful to allow a space for these doubts and questions. Often it is the character of Satan that articulates the reader's own hesitancy and perplexity as she reads the poem:

> … Knowledge forbidden?
> Suspicious, reasonless. Why should their Lord
> Envy them that? Can it be sin to know,
> Can it be death? And do they only stand
> By ignorance, is that their happy state …?   (IV, ll. 515–9)

The questions that dominate the movement of Satan's mind in the fourth book, questions that will form the substance of his temptation of Eve in Book IX, are the questions that must bother the reader as she interprets *Paradise Lost*. Can it really be sinful to desire god-like knowledge? Can it really bring spiritual death to mankind? Is ignorant obedience really the perfection of human freedom? Milton, characteristically, demands an active double-reading from us on each of these points. While the semantics of his questions seem sincere, Satan's designation of God as '*their* Lord', his idiosyncratic sibilance, and his use of the pejoratives 'envy', 'suspicious' and 'reasonless' with reference to God, all suggest a calculated quality to his questions which is not at all apparent at first reading. As Stanley Fish writes in his essay 'Discovery as Form in *Paradise Lost*' (1971), 'It is the reader who moves, or advances, until his cleansed eye can see what has always been there.' Milton's purpose in his grand epic is thus the gradual education of his readers to recognize and condemn evil, even when it is presented in as attractive and compelling a form as that of his Satan. We are encouraged to perceive Adam and Eve's standing before God at this stage in the poem as a dynamic trust which is infinitely preferable to Satan's furtive challenges.

FAITH AND APOSTASY

Milton's celebration of man's ability to stand before God both physically – as the pinnacle of God's creation made to rule over the animal kingdom – and spiritually – by the exercise of his will in obedience to God's commands – resounds through *Paradise Lost*. True innocence, for Milton, is found in nothing more (and certainly nothing less) than the action of standing before God in obedience. As the writer of the New Testament letter to the Ephesians exhorts believers to '... withstand in the evil day, and having done all, to stand. Stand therefore, having your loins girt about with truth' (Eph. 6:13–14, *RSV*), so Milton imagines Eve through Satan's eyes:

> ... Eve separate he spies,
> Veiled in a cloud of fragrance, where she stood,
> ... oft stooping to support
> Each flow'r of slender stalk, whose head though gay
> ... Hung drooping unsustained, them she upstays
> Gently with myrtle band, mindless the while,
> Herself, though fairest unsupported flow'r ...'   (IX, ll. 424–33)

The poet lingers over his almost motionless portrait of Eve in a single sentence that runs for 17 lines. Milton himself stands (in the sense of pausing or delaying) picturing Eve, in a terrible irony, as the 'fairest unsupported flow'r' in paradise. This first, and most beautiful, of all women is both 'veiled' by the fragrance of the flowers she tends and compared, by means of a linking rhyme 'oft stooping ... / ... Hung drooping', to their posture. In a keen moment of **prolepsis**, Milton moves quickly and awkwardly from the present tense of Satan who 'spies' Eve, to the past tense of 'where she stood'. That is to say, despite the fact that at this point

> **KEYWORD**
>
> Prolepsis: a figurative device by which a future occurrence is understood to have already happened.
>
> apostate: in Greek etymology this word literally signifies *to stand apart* from someone or something. It has now come to mean an abandonment of one's religious faith or moral principles.

in the poem Eve has not yet fallen into disobedience, Milton cannot maintain the present tense to write the grammatically consistent (but distressingly inappropriate) 'where she stands'. In the poet's mind, Eve's subsequent fall has contaminated even his image of her initial innocence.

The carefully constructed stasis of this scene contrasts to the devastatingly swift movements of Eve's fall:

> So saying, her rash hand in evil hour
> Forth reaching to the fruit, she plucked, she ate (IX, ll. 780–1)

With crashing monosyllabic certainty, Milton figures Eve's 'rash' movement towards her own fall. In the simple clauses dominated by the physical activities of saying, reaching, plucking and eating, Eve becomes the first human **apostate** from God. This culminating point of the poem, the point at which paradise is truly lost to the first man and woman, is thus the first moment of humanity's disobedient action towards God. After this, the mood of *Paradise Lost* changes from that of hope to nostalgia; after Adam has been persuaded to join Eve in her new knowledge, man and woman no longer stand in confident, naked obedience before God, but in covered, cowering and evasive rebellion.

It is fascinating to observe the movements of Milton's Satan throughout *Paradise Lost*: now falling, now flying, transporting himself in a frenzy of lawless, yet beautiful, activity. In Book IV of the poem, at a point when Milton allows Satan to stand still gazing at God's creation of the earth, something remarkable occurs:

> ... the sun
> Declined was hasting now with prone career
> To th'Ocean Isles, and in th'ascending scale
> Of heav'n the stars that usher evening rose:
> When Satan still in gaze, as first he stood,
> Scarce thus at length failed speech recovered sad.'   (*PL*, IV, ll. 352–7)

Although Satan is alliteratively linked to the sun, scale and stars, all of which are in a state of movement upwards, he stands in passive opposition to them, gazing at God's new act of creation with wistful longing. The poet again requires a double-reading from us as his ostensibly spatial comments on Satan's transfixed state, 'still in gaze', and 'as first he stood' in *space*, also have touching temporal implications: Satan is standing still in *time*, standing before God in a state of innocent rapture as he used to do. At this point in Milton's epic, Satan's posture thus reflects a momentary apostasy to his own evil, a standing apart from his own shame to wonder at creation and grieve for the paradise he has lost.

DYNAMIC STASIS: THE PERFECTION OF MAN IN ACTIVE OBEDIENCE

Milton's argument that man and woman can only come to perfection when they are in spiritual submission to their Creator, is extended in the poems *Paradise Regained* and *Samson Agonistes*. In these works, Milton moves his focus away from the original Fall and moral alienation of the first pair, to the possibilities for reuniting the human with the divine. In these poems of redemption (see Glossary), Milton makes it clear that enduring temptation and suffering in active obedience to God is infinitely preferable to a frenetic, and self-defeating, quest for power.

In *Paradise Regained*, Milton writes of Christ:

> To conquer Sin and Death the two grand foes,
> By humiliation and strong sufferance:
> His weakness shall o'ercome Satanic strength
> ...
> This perfect man, by merit called my Son,
> To earn salvation for the sons of men.   (I, ll. 159–61, 166–7)

The Christ of *Paradise Regained*, a perfect man, is able to overcome the strength of evil with the weakness and 'humiliation' of true obedience to God. As St Paul writes in his first letter to the Corinthians, 'God chose what is weak in the world to shame the strong' (1 Cor. 1:27, *RSV*). It is in this perfect obedience to God, suffering temptation and trial that Milton's Christ is able to 'earn salvation for the sons of men', that is, to regain the paradise of human communion with God by his willingness to endure even death for our sake. Once again, this willingness to submit is pictured by the poet in strikingly physical terms:

> ... ill wast thou shrouded then,
> O patient Son of God, yet only stood'st
> Unshaken; nor yet stayed the terror there,
> Infernal ghosts, and hellish furies, round
> Environed thee, some howled, some yelled, some shrieked,
> Some bent at thee their fiery darts, while thou
> Sat'st unappalled in calm and sinless peace.   (PR, IV, ll. 419–25)

As Christ endures another night of temptation in the desert, he is subjected by Satan to storms, ghosts and furies without number. Despite his lack of shelter or security, Christ's endurance is visualized as a posture of standing 'unshaken' against the wind and terror, or sitting 'unappalled' in serenity and peace. That is to say, although in exile, weak and vulnerable, Milton proposes that Christ's dynamic stasis, his vital stillness, is alone able to bring us back into a position of standing before God.

FREEDOM

Milton's commitment to the libertarian cause (see Biography) expressed itself not only in his political writings, but also in his poetry. His desire to see humanity freed from every form of slavery – intellectual, religious and political – motivated some of his finest writing. Yet, in Milton's mind, man comes to true freedom only by faith in, and obedience to, the Christian God. For example, as the morally fallen and despondent Adam prepares to leave his earthly paradise at the close of Milton's *Paradise Lost*, the Archangel Michael counsels him:

> ... only add
> Deeds to thy knowledge answerable, add faith,
> Add virtue, patience, temperance, add love,
> ... then wilt thou not be loath
> To leave this Paradise, but shalt possess
> A paradise within thee, happier far. (XII, ll. 581–7)

Milton's conception of true freedom thus involves a crucial paradox. Adam will lose his paradise only to gain it; by his free actions of faith and obedience to God and love towards man he will discover a 'paradise within' himself, 'happier' than that earthly paradise which he must leave. This theme of freedom with obedience (an ideal derived from the Gospel accounts of Christ's life) infuses much of Milton's poetry and lends to it a uniquely Christian character. In particular, *Paradise Lost*, *Paradise Regained* and *Samson Agonistes*, expanding on the insight that man must obey God in order to be truly free, tell us much about Milton's view of humanity within the divine scheme.

FREEDOM OF THE WILL

In writing about spiritual freedom as the perfection of human purpose, Milton was knowingly engaged in a debate that had raged in the Christian Church since its beginning: namely, does God allow human beings to make their own free choices and reap the unknown consequences of those choices, or is he a really a kind of divine puppeteer, pulling unseen strings to determine our every action? In the period of the European Reformation (see Historical, Political and Religious Contexts) this debate had re-emerged in the writings of John Calvin and Jacobus Arminius. While Calvin believed in man's **total depravity** and God's sovereign act of **predestination**, Arminius maintained that man had been given the **post-lapsarian** gift of free-will to choose his own destiny. As we might expect, on most theological issues Milton was staunchly Arminian in his outlook, and this Arminianism is reflected in his poetry.

In *Paradise Lost*, Milton dramatizes God's foreknowledge of man's Fall in the following way:

> … I made him just and right,
> Sufficient to have stood, though free to fall.
> Such I created all th'ethereal Powers
> And Spirits, both them who stood and them who failed;
> Freely they stood who stood, and fell who fell.
>   (PL, III, ll. 98–102)

The poet's skilful use of a medial **caesura** both in the line, 'Sufficient to have stood, though free to fall' and the line, 'Freely they stood who stood, and fell who fell', underscores his Arminian emphasis on free will, with the balance internal to each line indicating the equally possible but opposing choices of standing in obedience to God or falling into evil. Notice that Milton lets the words 'fall', 'failed' and 'fell' themselves fall on line endings, indicating God's displeasure at Satan's free decision to disobey him and fall into sin.

KEYWORDS

Total depravity: the belief that humanity is infected by sin in all of its faculties: *i.e.* the will, heart, mind and soul are all touched and tainted by human wickedness, making man incapable of achieving anything good without the help of a loving God.

Predestination: the doctrine that God fore-ordains, or elects, all of those that will choose to follow him.

Post-lapsarian: occurring after the Fall of Adam and Eve in the Genesis narratives of the Bible. According to Christian teaching, post-lapsarian humanity is not in the initial state of innocence in which the first man and woman existed.

Caesura: a pause or break in a line of poetry, often marked by punctuation.

Human liberty for Milton thus involves some element of free choice and, as *Paradise Lost* revolves around Adam and Eve's fall into the temptation of disobedience, so *Paradise Regained* celebrates Christ's resistance to the same temptation. These are the opening lines:

> I who erewhile the happy garden sung,
> By one man's disobedience lost, now sing
> Recovered Paradise to all mankind,
> By one man's firm obedience fully tried
> Through all temptation, and the tempter foiled ...   (I, ll. 1–5)

The Christ of *Paradise Regained*, who Barbara Lewalski describes as 'subject to doubts and fears, ... undergoing a genuine adventure of testing and self-discovery' (*Milton's Brief Epic*, 1966), is a Christ who Milton maintains is 'fully tried / Through all temptation'. This stress on the *humanity* of the Son is typical of Milton; his Christ is one who is able to bring humanity 'Recovered Paradise' precisely because he suffers human temptation and yet remains in firm obedience to God.

PERSONAL RESPONSIBILITY FOR FREE ACTIONS

Milton was anxious to illustrate that God's gift of free will, although enabling mankind to make its own spiritual decisions, also carries with it an enormous burden of personal responsibility for individual obedience. In *Samson Agonistes*, the poet stresses that man will be held accountable to God for all of his free actions and decisions (see Major works II: *Samson Agonistes*). The hero of the story is visited in prison by his old father, Manoa, who blames God for foreseeing but not preventing his son's fall. Samson replies to him:

> Appoint not heavenly disposition, father,
> Nothing of all these evils hath befall'n me
> But justly; I myself have brought them on,
> Sole author I, sole cause ...   (l.373–6)

By asserting that God's judgement upon him is just, Samson carefully distinguishes between divine foreknowledge and human freedom. In his claim to be 'author' of his own evil, the origin of his own misfortune, Samson echoes Milton's description of Satan in *Paradise Lost* as the 'author of all ill' (II, l.381). Samson's claim is also reminiscent of a long passage on the compatibility of free will and foreknowledge in Milton's later theological treatise *Christian Doctrine*, where he writes that '... neither God's decree nor his foreknowledge can shackle free causes with any kind of necessity' otherwise God would be made '... the cause and author of sin'. If we examine how Milton writes these lines – that is, if we examine the poetical devices he uses to achieve an effect – Samson's radical assumption of responsibility becomes even clearer. That Samson is made to describe his captivity and loss of strength as an adversity that has 'befall'n' him, reminds us that he is living after the Fall of man, and therefore tainted by human sin. In the words 'I myself have brought them on, / Sole author I, sole cause', Milton's elaborate wordplay on the ambivalent sounds of sole/soul and I/eye recalls us to the knowledge that evil has its origin in the human soul, and is eternally visible to an omniscient God.

---

* * *SUMMARY* * *

● It is rewarding to gain an awareness of Milton's technical artistry, paying attention to such poetic devices as metaphor, rhyme and wordplay in his work.

● Milton allows room for doubts and questions in his dramatization of the spiritual life.

● Milton's poetry often demands a second or third reading in order to appreciate its ambiguities.

7 Early Critical Approaches

RHYME

Strange as it may appear to us now, the central issue at stake for early literary critics of *Paradise Lost* was Milton's refusal to use rhyme. Calling it 'the invention of a barbarous age, to set off wretched matter and lame meter …', Milton saw rhyme as a positive hindrance to the writing of epic poetry in English, denouncing the 'jingling sound of like endings' (Preface to *Paradise Lost*) and espousing instead a freedom of verse which English poets have taken for granted ever since. Early critic, poet of much esteem, and friend to Milton, Andrew Marvell plants himself firmly on the side of those who approve of the poet's choice:

> Thou sing'st with so much gravity and ease;
> And above humane flight dost soar aloft
> With Plume so strong, so equal, and so soft …
> Thy Verse created like thy Theme sublime,
> In Number, Weight and Measure, needs not Rime
>
> ('On *Paradise Lost*' ll. 36–8, 53–4)

Although facetiously using rhyme himself to make the point, Marvell characterizes Milton's verse as so strong – like Satan in *Paradise Lost* 'soaring' in flight above its imitators – that rhyme would be an unnecessary adornment to it. Milton's adversary, John Dryden, was more straightforwardly cynical about the poet's refusal to use rhyme in his epic:

> … whatever causes he alleges for the abolishing of rhyme, (which I have not now the leisure to examine) his own particular reason is plainly this, that rhyme was not his talent; he had neither the ease of doing it, nor the graces of it …
>
> (*Original and Progress of Satire*, 1693)

By making Milton the liar in this way, asserting that a lack of talent – and not an **aesthetic** principle – was the poet's chief reason for avoiding rhyme, Dryden paves the way for other negative reviews of *Paradise Lost*, culminating in the twentieth century Milton Controversy headed by poet T. S. Eliot and critic F. R. Leavis (see Modern critical approaches).

> **KEYWORD**
>
> Aesthetic: derived from the Greek *aisthēta*, 'things perceptible by the senses', aesthetics has come to mean that which is related to the beautiful, or to the work of art.

EXQUISITELY ARTIFICIAL

Another point of contention for early reviewers of Milton's poems was his habitual use of artificial (and just plain difficult) constructions not usually found in English poems. Although sometimes lost on the modern reader who is often unequipped with a knowledge of ancient languages, Milton habitually employs sentence structures, phrases and idioms which would be more at home in ancient Latin or Greek poems than in his native language. While John Keats describes *Paradise Lost* as 'The most remarkable Production of the world – A northern dialect accommodating itself to Greek and Latin inversions and intonations' (Letter to the George Keatses, 24 September 1819), Alexander Pope, as early as 1723, laments this tendency in Milton's poems:

> ... in his speeches (where clearness above all is necessary) there is frequently such transposition and forced construction, that the very sense is not to be discovered without a second or third reading: and in this certainly he ought to be no example.'
>
> (Postscript to the *Odyssey*)

Today's reader, 300 years on and still struggling to find the verb in the very first (16 line) sentence in *Paradise Lost*, may take some comfort in Pope's exasperation! Other prominent poets and essayists, too, have expressed displeasure at Milton's style. Famously, Samuel Johnson, while valuing Milton's contribution to English poetry, found that with the poet's *Lycidas*, 'the diction is harsh, the rhymes uncertain and the numbers unpleasing', while *Paradise Lost*:

... is one of the books which the reader admires and lays down ... Its perusal is a duty rather than a pleasure. We read Milton for instruction, retire harassed and overburdened and look elsewhere for recreation.

(*Lives of the Poets*, 1779–81)

Unlike the **Romantic** critics that would soon follow him, Johnson tempers a cautious admiration of Milton's achievements with honesty about his dislike of the reading experience occasioned by his poetry. Milton, for Johnson, is talented but tiresome, reading his work is a 'duty' for the educated reader that leaves him 'harassed' and overworked. Compare this grudging commendation to the enthusiastic devotion of Romantic poet Coleridge, who remarks that Milton's style is '*exquisitely* artificial', and ordered to the

> **KEYWORD**
>
> Romantic: in England, the Romantic movement in literature is chiefly associated with the figures of Blake, Coleridge, Wordsworth, Keats, Shelley and Byron. A rejection of received standards and beliefs resulted in the Romantic emphasis on the primacy of creative freedom.

'language of passion' rather than to the 'logic of grammar' ('Fourteen Lectures for the London Philosophical Society', Lecture X, 1818). This very different assessment of Milton's worth as a poet is indebted in part to the Romantic notion that poetry should be celebrated as a vehicle for the 'spontaneous overflow of powerful feelings' (Wordsworth, Preface to *The Lyrical Ballads*, 1800). Such a transformation of critics' expectations concerning what poetry should do to its readers led to a shift in Milton criticism. From now on, the focus would be taken away from technical questions regarding Milton's style and placed instead upon assessments of character and conviction.

THE CLOUDED RUINS OF A GOD

In an extraordinary philosophical prose-work committed to the overthrow of conventional morality, *The Marriage of Heaven and Hell* (1790), William Blake added the famous observation on Milton that would forever re-shape literary opinion of *Paradise Lost* and its author:

Note: The reason Milton wrote in fetters when he wrote of Angels &
God, and at liberty when of Devils & Hell, is because he was a true poet
and of the Devil's party without knowing it.

Blake's radical claim – that Milton creates an inspiring, even majestic,
Satan in *Paradise Lost*, but that he becomes poetically strangled in his
treatment of the orthodox Christian God – must be conceded. It is fair
to say that the finest, most poignant, passages in *Paradise Lost* are
dedicated to, or spoken by, Satan himself. How can the reader account
for Milton's peculiar sympathy towards the Devil in his avowedly
Christian poem? For Blake, the answer is that Milton was 'of the Devil's
party without knowing it'. This is not to say that Blake considers Milton
to be a clandestine Satanist, but rather that he believes in *Paradise Lost*
the 'true poet' in Milton is struggling to articulate an unorthodox
vision and is thus drawn to the noble yet defiant figure of Satan.

Indeed, for those Romantic poets following Blake, interpretation of
Milton's Satan had become the fashionable topic in literary criticism.
For Shelley, poet, atheist and political rebel, Milton's Devil '... as a
moral being is ... far superior to his God,' because he continually and
energetically strives 'in spite of adversity and torture' towards his
ambition. In contrast, Milton's God is portrayed by Shelley as fighting
the Devil 'in the cold security of undoubted triumph' (*On the Devil,
and Devils*, 1819), immorally inflicting an 'enduring and terrible'
revenge upon him in the knowledge of his own assured victory. No
doubt Shelley's political views – he writes as a political radical and a
supporter of the French Revolution – were at play in this sympathetic
reading of Milton's Satan as one who challenges orthodox doctrine and
unsettles political conservatism.

For Samuel Taylor Coleridge, Romantic poet, essayist and Christian
theologian, Milton's creation of a proud, energetic and vigorous Devil
in *Paradise Lost* does not reveal his approval of Satan's rebellion against
God. Rather, Milton's Satan is perceived by Coleridge as a dazzling but
melancholy sinner, condemned to suffer in the hell of his own making:

Milton has carefully marked in his Satan the intense selfishness, the alcohol of egotism, which would rather reign in hell than serve in heaven … But around this character he has thrown a singularity of daring, a grandeur of sufferance, and a ruined splendour, which constitute the very height of poetic sublimity.

('Fourteen Lectures for the London Philosophical Society',
Lecture X, 1818)

Likewise, William Hazlitt confesses himself unimpressed by the argument that Milton was secretly devoted to the dissident yet resplendent figure of Satan. Just because '(t)he horns and tail are not there', he writes, does not mean that the poet did not attend to Satan's 'writhing agonies within'. Satan's ravaged grandeur, for Coleridge and Hazlitt, is thus to be pitied rather than admired. Refusing to create a caricature of evil, these writers believed that Milton has depicted instead in his Satan the moral and intellectual consequences of a life lived in **sin**. Hazlitt's memorable description of Milton's anti-hero, in all his ambivalence, can be viewed as the foundation for those twentieth-century readings of Satan which see the character as Milton's finest poetic achievement:

> **KEYWORD**
>
> Sin: a term used in Christian theology to denote a disrupted relationship with God. Typically characterized as stance of rebellion towards God, sin is best understood as that which is opposed to the reality of the good.

Wherever the figure of Satan is introduced, whether he walks or flies, 'rising aloft incumbent on the dusky air', it is illustrated with the most striking and appropriate images: so that we see it always before us, gigantic, irregular, portentous, uneasy, and disturbed – but dazzling in its faded splendour, the clouded ruins of a god.

(*On Shakespeare and Milton*, 1818)

* * * SUMMARY * * *

- Early critics debated whether Milton's refusal to use rhyme in *Paradise Lost* was due to his poetic originality and strength, or whether he simply lacked the talent for it.

- Milton's employment of Greek and Latin constructions in his poetry often frustrated his critics.

- For the Romantic poets and critics, Milton's characterization of Satan in *Paradise Lost* became a fashionable topic in literary criticism.

8 Modern Critical Approaches

For each poem ... ideally, there is distinguishable a logical object or universal ... The critic has to take the poem apart, or analyze it, for the sake of uncovering these features. With all the finesse possible, it is a rude and patchy business by comparison with the living integrity of the poem. But without it there could hardly be much understanding of the value of poetry.

('Criticism Inc.', John Crowe Ransom, *Virginia Quarterly Review*, 1937)

We might say that the task of criticism ... is purely formal; it does not consist in 'discovering' in the work or in the author under consideration something 'hidden' or 'profound' or 'secret' ... but only in *fitting together* – as a skilled cabinet maker ... the language of the day (Existentialism, Marxism, or psycho-analysis) and the language of the author.

('Criticism as Language', Roland Barthes, *The Critical Moment*, 1964)

Very broadly speaking, it is possible to distinguish two significant currents in twentieth-century criticism of Milton, the spirits of which are essentially captured in the excerpts reprinted above.

NEW CRITICISM

The first of these currents is that which has been absorbed by the techniques and assumptions of New Criticism – associated with British and American critics such as I. A. Richards, F. R. Leavis and Cleanth Brooks. New Criticism perceives the importance of a literary text to lie in the words on the page, and not in such external factors as the author's life, her intentions, the historical and intellectual context in which the work was written, or the reader's responses to the work. As such, New Critics and those influenced by them believe that criticism should dissect and scrutinze a literary text for the relationships between form and meaning within it. As Ransom writes, the critic must 'take the poem apart' or 'analyze it' in order to uncover its universal truth, or logical object. For the New Critic, then, the text is independent from historical or subjective factors and its meanings can be discovered and deciphered through meticulous attention simply to the words on the page. In this way, the New Critic of Milton sees himself as listening to the poem and, in doing so, the 'value of poetry' is both estimated in his work and becomes reborn in the work of the critic.

THEORY-LED CRITICISM

The second, more contemporary, current of criticism on Milton is that which has been informed by the abundance of social, political and linguistic critical theories which have flourished since the 1960s. Like the New Critic, the theory-led critic attempts to restate the poem or text in a critical language. What is crucial to note here, though, is that this other language is not the 'hidden' or 'secret' meaning of the text, discernible by scrupulous close-reading of the words on the page. Instead the language of the critic, his recreation of the text is, in Barthes's words, a 'fitting together' of his own language and the author's language. This dialogue between past text and present criticism will, moreover, be biased not towards the universal 'value of poetry' as such, but towards the critic's present articulation of it. As Barthes writes at the close of his essay, criticism is '... the ordering of that which is intelligible in our own time'. Unlike Ransom's New Critical approach to criticism in which timeless and universal truths are uncovered in literary artefacts, Barthes's insistence is thus upon the history, intellectual background and convictions ('Existentialism, Marxism, or psycho-analysis') which the critic brings with him to the text. For the theory-led critic, therefore, poetry can never be what it has been in the past, it can never be cleansed from its own history and politics, or from the history and politics intervening in the passage of time between its being written and read. Likewise, the text cannot be purified from gender-based and psychological factors – either those of the author or those of its readers.

ELIOT, LEAVIS AND THE MILTON CONTROVERSY

The most energetic, influential, and damaging period of Milton criticism in the twentieth century occurred in the critical writings of T. S. Eliot and F. R. Leavis. Later known as the Milton Controversy, the Eliot–Leavis attack on Milton depended upon the objectifying insights of New Criticism for its force. Eliot's essay 'The Metaphysical Poets', published for the first time in 1921, was the beginning of the assault in that it described true poetry – supremely that of John Donne – as that which dynamically unsettles the relationship between intellectual understanding and poetic form. According to Eliot, 'A thought to Donne was an experience; it modified his sensibility'. However, Eliot contended, later seventeenth-century poetry, and especially that of Milton, was subject to what he called a 'dissociation of sensibility', by which he meant that the poet's refinement of language, his grand, Latinate vocabulary and elevated style, gave rise to a separation in the poetry between thought and feeling. The heart of Eliot's critique lay in his contention that:

> To extract everything possible from *Paradise Lost*, it would seem necessary to read it in two different ways, first solely for the sound, and second for the sense … Now (in) Shakespeare, or Dante … (t)here is no interruption between the surface that these poets present to you and the core … I cannot feel that my appreciation of Milton leads anywhere outside of the mazes of sound.
>
> (*On Poetry and Poets*, 1957. First published 1936)

As New Criticism relies on close reading of literary texts to extract how their form and style relate to what Ransom called the universal meanings within them, so Eliot charged Milton with divorcing sound from sense. The meaning of this accusation is that, according to Eliot, Milton so successfully invents a poetic language of his own that the reader must separate the stylistic accomplishments of his poetry, its sound, from its meaning or sense. Shakespeare and Dante, on the other hand, are approved by Eliot as maintaining a true relationship between surface style and core meaning. In this way, Eliot declares that he finds himself lost in Milton's poetry, it fails to lead him towards a hidden meaning and instead leaves him inside what he describes as 'the mazes of sound', at the surface of the poetry. This belief that the style of poetry should enact its meaning would become heavily criticized by theory-led critics after the 1960s.

Eliot did revise his 1930s criticisms of Milton a decade later, admitting that although, '(t)he emphasis is on the sound, not on the vision, upon the word, not the idea', this concentration constitutes Milton's 'peculiar greatness' (1947). Yet the legacy of Eliot's initial attack would survive for several decades following his 1936 essay, and this survival must be traced substantially to the writings of New Critic F. R. Leavis. In his book *Revaluations*, published at the same moment as Eliot's 1936 essay, Leavis makes the startling claim that:

> Milton's dislodgement, in the past decade, after his two centuries of predominance, was effected with remarkably little fuss.

Leavis, like Eliot, goes on to argue that he finds himself fundamentally bewildered by Milton's unconventional use of English language in *Paradise Lost*, seeing it as 'a consistent rejection of English idiom', an aberration within what he calls the 'Great Tradition' of English literature. Particularly obnoxious to Leavis is the metrical arrangement, or music, of Milton's verse; the critic argues that the rhythms of Milton's blank verse in *Paradise Lost*, while admittedly varied and complex, leave him cold. As he remarks:

> (Milton) exhibits a feeling *for* words rather than a capacity for feeling *through* words; we are often, in reading him, moved to comment that he is 'external' or that he 'works from the outside'.

Again, like Eliot, Leavis distinguishes between Milton's 'feeling *for* words', his obvious enjoyment of their sounds and textures, and the aptitude in other poets for 'feeling *through* words', for making meanings transparent to the reader in the style of their poetry. Yet, the Eliot–Leavis critique of Milton presupposes that meaning really does reside inside poems and other texts, as something internal to them which can be discovered later by the critic as she takes them apart. This assumption becomes questioned by the theory-led critics who later refuse to read literature as a simple process of disclosure or uncovering. For the earlier New Critics, though, the disjointed relationship between style and meaning in Milton would remain a serious flaw of the Grand Style.

WALDOCK, EMPSON AND MILTON'S DOUBT

The strain between sounds and meanings that Eliot and Leavis perceived as a fault in Milton's poetry was viewed by other critics, even those influenced by the New Critical approach, as a demonstration of Milton's religious doubts. Both A. J. A. Waldock and William Empson would view these tensions not as symptomatic of Milton's failure to write good poetry but rather as internal evidence of the poet's unease with his own subject matter. Waldock asserted that in *Paradise Lost*:

> Adam cannot give Milton much scope to express what he really feels about life: but Satan is there, Satan gives him scope. And the result is that the balance is somewhat disturbed; pressures are set up that are at times disquieting, that seem to threaten more than once, indeed, the equilibrium of the poem.

> (*Paradise Lost and its Critics*, 1947)

For Waldock, influenced as he is by Blake and Shelley (see Early Critical Approaches), close reading of Milton's poems reveals a disturbance of balance, a pressure between form and meaning that gives him 'scope to express what he really feels about life'. Milton's portrayal of Satan was too luxurious and exciting, and his portrait of God too tyrannical and offensive, for a reader to credit the poet with absolutely orthodox Christian beliefs. Yet for Waldock, the tension that threatens the internal balance of the poem is not a fault, but an achievement of the poetry, evidence of its establishing a true relationship between sound and sense. In this way, by creating tremors and inconsistencies in the metrical arrangement, plot or characters of the poem, Waldock maintains that Milton is expressing his doubts about the orthodox Christian portrait of God.

William Empson, in his influential study *Milton's God* (1961), amplifies Waldock's reading of *Paradise Lost*, finding in the poem internal evidence of political and religious tensions which he believes mirror those in the poet's mind. In his analysis of the following lines from Book III of *Paradise Lost*, describing God's plans for Jesus Christ at the end of human history, Empson reaches some groundbreaking conclusions regarding Milton's theological beliefs:

> ... in thee
> Love hath abounded more than glory abounds,
> Therefore thy humiliation shall exalt
> With thee thy manhood also to this throne;
> Here shalt thou sit incarnate, here shalt reign
> Both God and man, Son both of God and man ...
> (*Paradise Lost*, III, 311-16)

Empson's analysis of these lines runs like this:

> It is a tremendous moral cleansing for Milton's God, after the greed for power which can be felt in him everywhere else, to say that he will give his throne to Incarnate Man, and the rhythm around the word *humiliation* is like taking off in an aeroplane.

Empson's careful close reading of Milton's lines brings to light a tension between the poet's style, his use of consistently high-stressed syllables in this passage, 'like taking off in an aeroplane', and his meaning, to show that God the Father will yield his throne to a human being at the end of history. Milton's God is thus shown to be both greedy for power, and yet capable of ultimate self-negation, and it is this tension within the poet's theology that comes to the surface of his poetry. As Empson concludes on these lines, 'Milton could never let the Father appear soft and his deepest yielding must be almost hidden by a blaze of glory'. For Waldock and Empson, then, Milton's poetry uniquely relates the technique of writing to the beliefs expressed by it; *Paradise Lost*, especially, invites the reader to actually experience Milton's religious doubts at first hand by encountering cracks and pressures in the style of the poem.

READER-RESPONSE CRITICISM

Empson and Waldock's exploration of what Richard Bradley calls the 'troubling relationship between what Milton wrote and the way he wrote it' (*The Complete Critical Guide to John Milton*, 2001), still relies on the New Critical assumption that the role of the critic is to uncover meanings deep within the poem itself. Stanley Eugene Fish's theory-led book *Surprised by Sin*, was to challenge that assumption within Milton studies, and propose that meaning is something the reader brings to her reading of Milton, not something she takes from it. Before Fish's book, very few critics gave much attention to the role of the reader in establishing the meaning of a text. In fact, New Critics W. K. Wimsatt and Monroe C. Beardsley scathingly labelled any such identification of the poem and its results – 'what it *is* and what it *does*' – the 'affective fallacy' (*The Verbal Icon: Studies in the Meaning of Poetry*, 1954). Refusing to obey the New Criticism's demand for critical objectivity, Fish argues that in *Paradise Lost*, 'Milton's method is to recreate in the mind of the reader the drama of the Fall, to make him fall again as Adam did' (*Surprised by Sin*, 1967). According to Fish, Milton's reader finds the figure of Satan mentally attractive and, in this way, actually re-enacts the process of temptation and Fall narrated in the poem. But the experience of reading *Paradise Lost* is not, in Fish's mind, simply reducible to this Romantic interpretation of Satanic temptation; rather the poem moves the reader from temptation to Fall and finally to **grace** by teaching her how to

KEYWORD

Grace: a term within Christian theology used to describe God's free and loving relationship with his creation. Ultimately, in the New Testament writings from which Milton was constantly drawing, grace is described as the revelation of God in Jesus Christ to liberate humanity from the consequences of the Fall.

recognize and become immune to the Satanic appeal. As Fish writes in his essay 'Discovery as form in Paradise Lost':

> It is important to realize that the poem does not move to this revelation; it has been there from the first, plainly visible to the eye capable of seeing it. It is the reader who moves, or advances, until his cleansed eye can see what has always been there.' (1971)

Fish's method opened up a rich new mine of interpretation within Milton studies. No longer were critics discouraged from openly acknowledging their own theoretical starting points (e.g. feminist, Marxist, psycho-analytic), and no longer were they encouraged to achieve critical 'objectivity'. Rather, the work of interpretation became seen as inextricably bound to the reader, her preferences, prejudices and presuppositions. By bringing literary criticism 'out of the closet' in this way, in allowing critics to confess their own intellectual starting points, Fish had created a new mode of literary criticism which became known as the 'reader-response' school, or 'reception' theory.

FEMINIST CRITICISM OF *PARADISE LOST*

By writing criticism that focused upon the dynamic experiences of the reader confronting Milton's texts, Fish opened the way for other theory-led schools of criticism to flourish. These approaches, including feminist, psycho-analytic, Marxist and deconstructive criticism, encourage a view of literature which is capable of attending to the sheer variety of readers accessing Milton's work. For the feminist interpreter, Fish's insight that the reader's experience will fundamentally affect her understanding of Milton's poems, means that the critic should emphasize how a reader's **gender** will change her personal reading of these texts.

KEYWORD

Gender: while a person's sex is determined by biological difference, their gender – the traits that determine masculinity and femininity – is constructed by upbringing and environment, culture and society. For feminist critics, the masculine gender has, in the West, come to be identified as practical, commanding, brave, rational and creative; while the feminine, by contrast, has come to be identified as intuitive, passive, modest, emotional and conformist.

As Milton portrays Adam lamenting his own Fall in the tenth book of *Paradise Lost*, he makes him cry,

> O why did God,
> Creator wise, that peopled highest heav'n
> With Spirits masculine ...
> ... not fill the world at once
> With men as angels without feminine?   (X. ll. 889–93)

To try and determine whether Adam's cry is the bitter outpouring of a broken spirit or whether, in some ways, his sentiment also belongs to Milton, has been one of the tasks of feminist criticism within Milton studies. Such criticism presupposes that our society is fundamentally ordered in the favour of men in all its spheres: religious, economic, political and legal. Furthermore, feminist critics allege that our culture's patriarchal philosophy also permeates its literature, even at the level of plot and characterization.

For feminist critics of Milton, therefore, two questions have generally predominated: whether and how his poetry reflects seventeenth-century attitudes towards women, and how we can interpret his characterization of Eve within *Paradise Lost*.

Critics such as Marcia Landy, James D. Simmonds, and Sandra K. Gilbert deny that Milton's poetry has escaped the influence of his upbringing or education. Instead, these critics concentrate on Milton's portrayal of Eve in *Paradise Lost* as a symbol of his **misogynist** views, alleging that the first female is presented purely as a by-product of Adam, a non-man. In this way, early feminist critics of Milton's work denounce *Paradise Lost* as a product of Milton's patriarchal imagination, an oppressive and domineering text that must be censured by the twentieth-century reader in order to be understood by her.

> **KEYWORD**
>
> Misogynist: literally *hater of women.*

Barbara K. Lewalski, in her pointed reply to Landy, complains that, rather than freeing Milton studies to pursue valuable insights, '... the ideology of feminism as a broader movement can cloud, sometimes deliberately obscure, the objective detail of literary scholarship' (*Milton Studies*, 6, 1974). Lewalski views *Paradise Lost* as a product of its time, a product which we should not attempt to read with twenty-first-century glasses. Rather, by studying views on gender and marriage which are contemporary to Milton, we should be able to achieve a more accurate and objective picture of the poet's opinions and intentions. For Lewalski, in *Paradise Lost* Milton has given the reader a liberal seventeenth-century portrait of Puritan marriage in which Eve is Adam's companion and aid; each has 'the need for the other, the inescapable bonds of human interdependence', and each is the other's spiritual complement.

Likewise, Diane Kelsey McColley in her defence of Milton's portrayal of Eve in *Paradise Lost*, counters the early feminist critique of Milton by maintaining that it is irrational to impose twentieth-century ideals on seventeenth-century literature. Milton, she writes, '... could neither be expected to rewrite Genesis completely nor to personally reschedule the seventeenth-century notion of the woman's social role.' (*Milton's Eve*, 1983). The critic Joseph Wittreich, writing in 1987, went even further in his assessment of Milton's contribution to the historical debate about gender roles within literature. In a daring book, *Feminist Milton*, Wittreich suggests that, in his deconstruction of 'dominant male patterns of thought' within *Paradise Lost*, Milton can actually be viewed as an 'early sponsor' of feminism. Wittreich's thesis depends on deconstructive techniques in order to maintain this insistence on the poem's ability to disturb settled assumptions about its meaning.

One of the most convincing feminist studies on Milton's poetry, is that of Janet E. Halley, 'Female Autonomy in Milton's Sexual Poetics' (*Milton and the Idea of Woman*, ed. Julia M. Walker, 1988). Accepting that the term 'feminist' has come to mean different things within Milton scholarship, referring both to those who perceive Eve to be simply a caricature of woman, an object of Milton's patriarchal fantasy, and those who believe that she is a fully rounded and autonomous character within the poem, Halley proposes a way through the dilemma. By uniting other critics' contrary insights that Eve is both autonomous and dependent on Adam in *Paradise Lost*, Halley maintains that 'female autonomy is given a contradictory structure' within the poem. Illustrating this point, Halley quotes from Book IV of *Paradise Lost*, when Eve tells the story of how she first fell in love with Adam, 'with that thy gentle hand / Seized mine, I yielded' (IV. 488–9). Halley argues that the balance in these lines between Adam's 'violent appropriation of her' (in 'seized') and 'her active, reasoning assent to it' (in 'yielded'), demonstrates Eve's place within the poem as a female figure who must both 'participate within the text, as a harmonic "other half"' and yet whose ultimate meaning as a female subject 'originates in male intention'.

DECONSTRUCTIONIST CRITICISM

The methods of criticism above, both those which are influenced by New Criticism and those which are theory-led, discuss Milton's poems as though their object lay in the transmission of meaning. For the New Critics, including Leavis and Eliot, meaning resides within the text itself, in the words on the page; Waldock and Empson, although influenced by New Criticism, locate the meaning of Milton's poems in the poet's doubts or beliefs; for reader-response and feminist criticisms a poem means something only when the reader interacts dynamically with it, bringing to it her own experiences. Yet this common assumption, that it is meaning the critic must search for either in the poem, the author, or the reader, has been radically questioned by deconstructionist criticism. Put very simply, deconstructionism is a way of understanding language that has evolved from certain insights of the early twentieth-century linguist Ferdinand de Saussure. In his *Course in General Linguistics* (1915), Saussure inaugurated what became known as the Structuralist school of linguistics by arguing that language does not act as an instrument to transmit reality, to communicate pre-existing meanings which are somehow out there in the world, but rather that individual words behave as signs which come to mean something only by virtue of their difference from other signs within the *structure* of a given language. 'Apple', that is, only means apple by virtue of the fact that English speakers have collectively agreed to assign it, and not the word 'banana', that function; there is no natural or intrinsic connection between the shape and sound of a word and its meaning, even if our routine use of language leads us to suppose that there is. As Roy Harris and Talbot J. Taylor write: 'Saussure's theory of *langue* [language] emerges as being rather like a theory of architecture according to which individual bricks only come into existence once the whole building is in place.' (*Landmarks in Linguistic Thought*, 1989).

Structuralist linguistics has changed the landscape of modern literary criticism because it has questioned the premise that language enables us to communicate meaning that already exists in the world. The Saussurean separation between the shape or sound of a sign (the *signifier*) and its meaning (that which is *signified*), has led to the more radically challenging insights of deconstruction, a theory-led movement begun by French philosopher Jacques Derrida, which flatly denies that language is capable of demonstrating any kind of meaning. In terms of its application to literary studies in general, and Milton criticism in particular, deconstructionist criticism attempts to demonstrate how texts themselves actually subvert – that is overthrow or undermine – their own claim to reflect meaning. As deconstructionist critic J. Hillis Miller writes:

> The deconstructive critic seeks to find ... the element in the system studied which is alogical, the thread in the text in question which will unravel it, or the loose stone which will pull down the whole building ... Deconstruction is not a dismantling of the structure of a text but a demonstration that it has already dismantled itself.
>
> ('Steven's Rock and Criticism as Cure, II,' *The Georgia Review*, 30, 1976)

In Milton studies, the deconstructionists' accusation that the poems, like all texts, ultimately dismantle themselves has been directed at the so-called impossibility of Milton's whole enterprise. That is to say, the poet's stated aims in writing *Paradise Lost*, namely '... to justify the ways of God to men' is doomed to fail because, according to deconstructionist critic Catherine Belsey:

> Whatever words are invoked to define him, God cannot be contained there. He is beyond difference itself ... God is different from everything we know, and therefore 'unspeakable', 'beyond thought'.   (1988)

Belsey sees the 'loose stone' in the building of *Paradise Lost* as its effort to do the impossible: to portray or defend an infinite God by using only finite human language. Because God is absolutely different to us, according to Belsey, we cannot possibly write about him in a way that will stand up to the deconstructionist critique and, in this way, the edifice of Milton's intention to transmit religious meaning is pulled down. For Belsey, a poem as ambitiously religious as *Paradise Lost* will be the cause of its own undoing as it will ultimately make it clear that language is not capable of telling the truth or transmitting meaning in any way. Yet Milton, writing some hundreds of years before deconstructionist criticism, saw very clearly both the limits of language in describing a transcendent God and the unsettling relationships between poetry and belief, fiction and doubt. As Richard Bradford writes:

> Milton was not a deconstructer. He was a Christian poet who was probably given to doubt the very basis of his beliefs, and as such he at least attended to the same agenda as poststructuralism – what exactly constitutes the real, the assumed and the represented.   (*ibid*)

✳ ✳ ✳ *SUMMARY* ✳ ✳ ✳

Modern critics approach Milton's work from a variety of different perspectives:

● New Critics, such as Eliot and Leavis, criticize Milton for a disjunction between the 'sound' and 'sense' of his poetry, while Waldock and Empson argue that tensions within the poetry demonstrate Milton's doubts about his own religious convictions;

● Reader-response criticism has become highly influential in Milton studies, proposing that meaning is brought by the reader *to* their reading of Milton, and not taken away *from* it;

● Feminist critics focus on Milton's adherence to seventeenth-century attitudes towards women and his characterization of Eve in *Paradise Lost*;

● Those critics influenced by the philosophy of Deconstruction endeavour to demonstrate that Milton's poems ultimately dismantle their own attempts to transmit stable meanings.

9 Where to Next?

Depending on the interests in Milton you have developed so far, there are many possible directions in which to turn next.

OTHER POETRY

Important among Milton's other poems, and falling outside the scope of this Beginner's Guide, are his early masque *Comus*, his verse elegy *Lycidas*, the poetic debating exercises of *L'Allegro* and *Il Penseroso*, the *Sonnets* and his meticulous translations of the *Psalms*. It is lamentable, especially in the case of *Lycidas*, that space does not permit detailed discussion.

John Carey's excellent collection *Milton: Complete Shorter Poems* (1968) contains all of these works, and many more besides.

PROSE

To get a flavour of Milton's political prose, you would be well advised to read the generous selections in Scott Elledge's Norton edition of *Paradise Lost* (1975, 1993) in which excerpts from *The Doctrine and Discipline of Divorce*, *Areopagitica*, *The Ready and Easy Way to Establish a Free Commonwealth* and *Christian Doctrine* are included. For the full texts of *Areopagitica* and *Of Education*, consult the Everyman edition of Milton's poems (*Complete English Poems*, ed. Gordon Campbell, 1993).

BIOGRAPHY

Milton's life story makes fascinating reading and there are many accessibly written biographies on the market. Highly recommended to read in tandem are A. N. Wilson's portrait of the poet *The Life of John Milton*, which portrays Milton as a political and religious conservative, and Christopher Hill's *Milton and the English Revolution*, which claims that he is anything but.

Barbara Lewalski's recent scholarly biography *The Life of John Milton* is a remarkable contribution to Milton biography which has the dual advantages of being beautifully written and not too heavily dependent on any one school of interpretation.

The earliest – and variably reliable – biographies of the poet are written by Aubrey (1681), Wood (1691), Phillips (1694) and Toland (1698). You can access these works in Helen Darbishire's useful collection *The Early Lives of John Milton* (1932).

CRITICISM

As you might imagine, there is a huge corpus of critical literature on Milton. Once again, Scott Elledge's edition of *Paradise Lost* is a good place to start as it includes several important contemporary essays on Milton as well as judicious selections from the work of earlier critics. Further recommendations for introductory reading include:

* Richard Bradford, *The Complete Critical Guide To John Milton* (2001)

* Lois Potter, *A Preface To Milton* (1986)

* Margarita Stocker, *Paradise Lost: The Critics Debate* (1988)

* William Zunder, *Paradise Lost. New Casebooks* (1999)

OTHER MEDIA

One very good way to get to know *Paradise Lost* is to listen to the poem being read aloud. The version currently available on audiobook is read by Anton Lesser, John Jenkins and Marin Marais (Naxos audiobooks, 1994).

Visual materials on Milton include the beautiful Victorian illustrations of *Paradise Lost* by Fuseli, Blake, Turner and Doré. You may find it interesting to view a selection on the web at www.stedwards.edu/hum/klawitter/milton/icon.htm.

L'Allegro and *Il Penseroso* have both been set to music by the composer Georg Friederich Handel. Worth finding and listening to is the Bach Choir and Paris Orchestral Ensemble's wonderful recording of these pieces, conducted by John Nelson and released on CD by Virgin Classics.

Chronology of Major Works

1629–32 *L'Allegro* and *Il Penseroso* probably written.

1634 *Comus* performed.

1637 *Comus* published.

1638 *Lycidas* printed in a collection of poems *Justa Eduardo King*.

1643 *Doctrine and Discipline of Divorce* published.

1644 *Of Education* and *Areopagitica* both published.

1645–6 *Poems of Mr John Milton, Both English and Latin ... 1645* registered and published.

1649 *On the Tenure of Kings and Magistrates* and *Eikonoklastes* published.

1655–6 Possibly starts to write *Christian Doctrine* and *Paradise Lost*.

1660 *A Ready and Easy Way to Establish a Free Commonwealth* published.

1665 Shows a friend the manuscript of *Paradise Lost*.

1667 *Paradise Lost* published in ten books.

1670 *History of Britain* published.

1671 *Paradise Regained* and *Samson Agonistes* published in the same volume.

1673 *Poems, &c. upon Several Occasions ... 1673* published.

1674 Second edition of *Paradise Lost* published in 12 books.

GLOSSARY

Aesthetic   Derived from the Greek aisthēta, 'things perceptible by the senses', aesthetics has come to mean that which is related to the beautiful, or to the work of art.

Apostate   In Greek etymology this word literally signifies *to stand apart* from someone or something. It has now come to mean an abandonment of one's religious faith or moral principles.

Blank verse   This verse form consists of unrhymed lines, ten beats long, usually in iambic meter. Closest to the natural cadences of English speech, blank verse is the most widely-used of verse forms in English poetry and drama.

Caesura   A pause or break in a line of poetry, often marked by punctuation.

Cosmology   That branch of science which deals with the origin and structure of the universe.

Epic   A long narrative poem on a grand and serious subject, narrated in a lofty style, often incorporating battles, legends and the supernatural. Belonging to this genre (in Greek) is Homer's *Iliad* and (in Latin) Virgil's *Aeneid*.

European Reformation   A complex of events and movements in the sixteenth century instigated by a German priest, Martin Luther, and aimed at reforming the Roman Catholic church.

Gender   While a person's sex is determined by biological difference, their gender – the traits that determine masculinity and femininity – is constructed by upbringing and environment, culture and society. For feminist critics, the masculine gender has, in the West, come to be identified as practical, commanding, brave, rational and creative; while the feminine, by contrast, has come to be identified as intuitive, passive, modest, emotional and conformist.

Grace   A term within Christian theology used to describe God's free and loving relationship with his Creation. Ultimately, in the New Testament writings from which Milton was constantly drawing, grace is described as the revelation of God in Jesus Christ to liberate humanity from the consequences of the Fall.

Hero Neither entirely good nor entirely evil, Aristotle says that a good tragic hero should be a fusion of both. Traditionally, the tragic hero should be more honourable than we ourselves are, in order that his fall from happiness to misery – due to an error of judgement or mistaken act – should move us to pity and fear.

Homoeopathic A branch of medicine in which patients are given small doses of salts, drugs etc. which would in a healthy person cause symptoms of the disease itself.

Idolatry The worship of an image or representation of God rather than the worship of God himself.

Independent Independents rejected the need for a State church and believed instead that Protestant sects should co-exist in a spirit of mutual toleration and respect for each other's religious freedom.

Messiah In the Hebrew Scriptures, the Messiah is the one promised to deliver the Jewish nation from oppression.

Metaphor A figure of speech in which one thing is described in terms of another. Particularly important for religious language, metaphor often enables us to speak of those things which lie outside our direct, everyday experience.

Meter From the Greek for *measure*, meter refers to the regular pattern of beats, the rhythmical variation of stressed and unstressed syllables, in poetry.

Misogynist Literally *hater of women*.

Muse The Muses were the nine daughters of Zeus in classical Greek mythology, each of whom presided over one art form. It is traditional for an epic poet to appeal to a particular Muse to help him write his work.

Oxymoron   A figure of speech which combines incongruous and apparently contradictory words and meanings for a special effect.

Patroness   One who uses her money and influence to support worthy people.

Post-lapsarian   Occurring after the Fall of Adam and Eve in the Genesis narratives of the Bible. According to Christian teaching, post-lapsarian humanity is not in the initial state of innocence in which the first man and woman existed.

Predestination   The doctrine that God fore-ordains, or elects, all of those that will choose to follow him.

Presbyterian   The Presbyterians were distinguished from other Puritan movements by their belief that church government should be organized by a Synod of Presbyters, both on a local and national level.

Prolepsis   A figurative device by which a future occurrence is understood to have already happened.

Protestantism   An umbrella term referring to the denominations emerging from Roman Catholicism during the Reformation. Included within it in Milton's time were the Puritan, Presbyterian and Independent sects.

Providence   A term used to express God's ongoing care and love for his creation.

Puritan   The Puritan movement was designed to restore to the churches the simplicity of the Christian religion as it is described in the gospel narratives of the Bible. Puritan emphases included the sovereignty of God over all human affairs and the use of everyday language for prayer.

Redemption   Deliverance from a state of slavery. In theology the term is used to denote Christ's deliverance of humankind from sin.

Romantic   In England, the Romantic movement in literature is chiefly associated with the figures of Blake, Coleridge, Wordsworth, Keats, Shelley and

Byron. A rejection of received standards and beliefs resulted in the Romantic emphasis on the primacy of creative freedom.

Sibilance   An alliterative repetition and playing upon the letter 's', usually at the beginning of words or stressed syllables in poetry.

Sin   A term used in Christian theology to denote a disrupted relationship with God. Typically characterized as stance of rebellion towards God, sin is best understood as that which is opposed to the reality of the good.

Soliloquy   From the Latin *solus* 'alone' and *loqui* 'to speak', a soliloquy is a speech, often extensive in length, uttered by a character who is alone on the stage. In drama and dramatic poetry, the soliloquy allows a writer the opportunity to convey a character's inmost thoughts, feelings and motivations.

Total depravity   The belief that humanity is infected by sin in all of its faculties, *i.e.* the will, heart, mind and soul are all touched and tainted by human wickedness, making man incapable of achieving anything good without the help of a loving God.

FURTHER READING

Benet, Diana Treviño and Michael Lieb, eds., *Literary Milton: Text, Pretext, Context* (Duquesne University Press, 1995)

Corns, Thomas N., ed., *A Companion to Milton* (Oxford, 2001)

Empson, William, *Milton's God* (1961; Cambridge: Cambridge University Press, 1981)

Fish, Stanley E., *Surprised by Sin: The Reader in Paradise Lost* (1967; Berkeley, CA: University of California Press, 1971)

Fish, Stanley, *How Milton Works* (Cambridge, MA, 2001)

French, J. Milton, ed., *The Life Records of John Milton*, 5 vols (1949–58).

Gilbert, Sandra, 'Patriarchal Poetry and Women Readers: Reflections on Milton's Bogey' *PMLA*, 93 (1978); reprinted in S. Gilbert and S. Gubar, *The Madwoman in the Attic*

Hill, Christopher, *Milton and the English Revolution* (London: Faber and Faber, 1977)

Hunter, G. K. (ed.), *A Milton Encyclopedia*, 9 vols., Lewisburg.

Knoppers, Laura, *Historicizing Milton: Spectacle, Power, and Poetry in Restoration England* (Athens: University of Georgia Press, 1994)

Lewalski, Barbara K., *Milton's Brief Epic: The Genre, Meaning, and Art of 'Paradise Regained'* (Providence: Brown U. P., 1966)

Lewalski, Barbara K., *The Life of John Milton* (Oxford, 2001).

Lewis, C. S., *A Preface to Paradise Lost* (London: Oxford University Press, 1942)

Lieb, Michael, *Milton and the Culture of Violence* (Cornell University Press, 1994)

Lieb, Michael and John T. Shawcross, eds., *Achievements of the Left Hand: Essays on the Prose of John Milton* (Amherst, MA: Massachusetts University Press, 1974)

Loewenstein, David, *Representing Revolution in Milton and His Contemporaries: Religion, Politics, and Polemics in Radical Puritanism* (Cambridge, 2001)

Norbrook, David *Poetry and Politics in the English Renaissance* (Oxford: Oxford University Press, 2002)

Masson, David, *The Life of John Milton*, 7 vols. (London: Macmillan, 1859-94).

Nicolson, Marjorie Hope, *John Milton: A Reader's Guide to His Poetry* (London: Thames and Hudson, 1964)

A. Patterson, ed., *John Milton* (Longman, 1992)

Ricks, Christopher, *Milton's Grand Style* (Oxford: Oxford University Press, 1963)

Rumrich, John P., *Milton Unbound: Controversy and Reinterpretation* (New York: Cambridge University Press, 1996)

Shawcross, John T., ed., *John Milton: The Critical Heritage*, 2 vols. (London: Routledge, 1970; reprinted 1995)

Turner, James Grantham, *One Flesh: Paradisal Marriage and Sexual Relations in the Age of Milton* (Oxford: Clarendon Press, 1987)

Wittreich, Joseph A., ed., *Calm of Mind: tercentenary essays on Paradise Regained and Samson Agonistes in honor of John S. Diekhoff* (Cleveland: Case Western University Press, 1971)

Wittreich, Joseph, *Interpreting Samson Agonistes* (Princeton, NJ: Princeton University Press, 1986)

Wolfe, Don M., ed., *Complete Prose Works of John Milton*, 8 vols., (New Haven and London: Yale University Press, 1953–82)

Worden, Blair, 'Milton, *Samson Agonistes*, and the Restoration', in Gerald MacLean, ed. *Culture and Society in the Stuart Restoration: Literature, Drama, History* (Cambridge: Cambridge University Press, 1985), 111–36

INDEX